W0009527

# CLANS AND TARTANS OF SCOTLAND

## RODDY MARTINE

BIRLINN

First published in 2022 by
Birlinn Ltd
West Newington House
10 Newington Road
Edinburgh
EH9 1QS

www.birlinn.co.uk

ISBN 978 1 78027 774 5

*British Library Cataloguing-in-Publication Data*
A catalogue record for this book is available
on request from the British Library

Designed and typeset by Mark Blackadder

Printed and bound by Gutenberg Press Ltd, Malta

# CONTENTS

# INTRODUCTION

'Clan' (the Gaelic word for 'family') is synonymous with Scottish antecedents the world over. However, it is important to differentiate between the clans of the Scottish Highlands and Islands and west country (Gaelic speaking), and the houses and families of Lowland Scotland (largely fluent in the dialects of old Scots, Doric and Lallans), now all collectively known as clans.

The former are predominantly of Celtic and Norse origin, whereas the latter are, in the majority, of Saxon and Norman descent. In this listing we feature only those clans where a Chief of the Name and Arms has been confirmed by the Lord Lyon King of Arms. Clans such as Anderson, Douglas and Stewart currently do not have recognised chiefs and are known as armigerous clans.

The prefix Mac indicates 'son of' in Gaelic and as such is widely dispersed north of the Highland line (loosely described as the territory north and west of the Grampian Mountains), and the islands of the Inner and Outer Hebrides situated off the west coast. Surnames found on Orkney and Shetland – and indeed in Caithness and Sutherland – more often than not display

Scandinavian influences, while the majority of traditional surnames found throughout the Lowlands, and across the Scottish Borders, from Berwickshire on the east coast to Dumfries and Galloway on the west coast, indicate Norman, Saxon or Germanic origins.

While all of these medieval clans/families have a number of extended family members (through descent or intermarriage), a significant number of their dependants or followers simply originate from the same territories within the Highlands and Islands, or from the Lowlands, mostly south of the Clyde and Forth estuaries.

The weaving of cloth was commonplace throughout the medieval world, but in the Highlands of Scotland, as opposed to the Lowlands, the colours of local plants, heathers and berries were imaginatively introduced into the manufacture of plaid, the everyday domestic garb of the Highland Scot, comprising striped patterns which eventually became known as tartan. Whereas some specific patterns and colours were considered territorial, and thus popular with certain clans, individual patterned cloth was never claimed exclusively by individual clans until the late 19th century.

The wearing of clan tartan, alongside the playing of bagpipes, was proscribed by the Dress Act of 1746, introduced after the Jacobite defeat at Culloden. The intention was to strike a death knell to the rebellious Highland tribal way of life with its clan allegiances and dependencies on ancestral chiefs holding political sway over clan territories. To a great extent this was successful.

It was largely the Catholic clans of the Highlands and Islands who supported the Jacobite Risings of 1689, 1715, 1719 and 1745. From 1746, it was decreed by the

Dress Act that imprisonment for six months was the punishment for 'anyone other than officers and soldiers in His Majesty's Forces (The Black Watch) caught wearing the plaid, philibeg, or little kilt, trowse, shoulder belts, or any part whatsoever of what peculiarly belongs to Highland garb; and that no tartan or party-coloured plaid or stuff shall be used for great coats, or for upper coats'.

It was not until 1782 that the Highland Society of London finally persuaded King George III to give his Royal assent to the ban being lifted to enable clan tartans to be revived.

Before the Jacobite Risings of the 17th and 18th centuries, many of the traditional tartan patterns we have come to know and love were already in existence, but styles of plaid were never considered exclusive or representative of one group or another. There are several examples of fashion-conscious Highlanders wearing more than one patterned plaid. Protestant Lowlanders mostly shunned Highland dress.

All that changed in 1822 when King George IV made his historic state visit to Edinburgh. No British monarch had set foot in Scotland for two centuries and, inspired by the widely admired Ossian poems of James Macpherson and romantic historical novels of Sir Walter Scott, it was as if every prosperous landowning family throughout Scotland needed to acquire a personalised tartan overnight.

Several were simply purchased off the peg from travelling haberdashers, but in no way does this belittle their eventual antiquity or lack of symbolic relevance. Even Prince Albert, the Prince Consort and husband of Queen Victoria, in 1853 was inspired to design and patent his very own Balmoral tartan.

As clan and family societies evolved in the years thereafter, and as further family groupings gained followings and official recognition, there was in some instances a demand to have more than one family tartan to wear. Thus some of the larger clans – Cameron, Campbell, Macdonald, MacLachlan, MacLeod, Sinclair, etc. –introduced Hunting, Dress, Ancient and Modern tartans, thus affording choices for informal every-day and formal evening wear.

Although it has been transported around the planet by the mass migration of Highland Scots to populate the New World, tartan fabric remains unique to Scotland, and it is universally recognised and lovingly cherished in its place of origin. We have here a decorative product that inspires patriotism, pride and loyalty wherever it is seen.

Since the 20th century, tartan has also been globally adapted for all kinds of decorative and commercial uses – domestic, corporate and industrial – thus creating a need to protect its authenticity. The thread count of every officially established tartan is therefore registered with the Scottish Register of Tartans, a charity established under the legal auspices of the Court of the Lord Lyon King of Arms, which alone is authorised to grant authenticity to the national dress of Scotland.

The Scottish Tartans Authority is a registered charity formed in 1996 and features on its website (www.tartanauthority.com) the most extensive collection of woven tartan samples in existence.

The majority of fabrics reproduced in this book are a mix of modern and ancient, the former more vibrant in its colours. The latter, being originally woven with vegetable dyes, is therefore subtly paler in comparison.

In the production of this book, the author and publisher are extremely indebted to the leading Highland Dress suppliers, Kinloch Anderson Scotland (www.kinlochanderson.com), for permission to reproduce their tartan samples.

Roddy Martine
Edinburgh
January 2022

# AGNEW

**Chief of the Name and Arms:**
Sir Crispin Agnew of Lochnaw Bt, LVO, QC, FRGS
**Motto**: 'By wisdom not by force' (*'Consilio non impetu'*)
**Crest:** An eagle issuing, regardant proper

A family of Norman origin which took its name from the Baronie d'Agneaux in north-west France. The surname first appears in Scotland in Liddesdale around 1190. In 1426, Sir Andrew Agnew was appointed Constable of Lochnaw Castle and in 1451 he was confirmed as Hereditary Sheriff of Wigtown. Sir Patrick, 8th Sheriff, and a member of the Scottish Parliament, was created a Baronet of Nova Scotia in 1625.

Supporters of the Stewart dynasty, Patrick Agnew, 4th of Lochnaw, died of wounds following the Battle of Flodden in 1513. Andrew, 5th of Lochnaw, was killed at the Battle of Pinkie in 1547. Sir Andrew, 5th Baronet, commanded the 21st Foot (later Royal Scots Fusiliers) against the French at the Battle of Dettingen in 1743 and during the Jacobite Rising of 1745 he held Blair Castle, seat of the Duke of Atholl, for the Hanoverians.

A branch of the family arrived in Ulster and were granted lands near Larne by James VI. Their castle, Kilwaughter, is now a ruin but many families in the USA and Australia descend from this line.

## ANCESTRAL INTEREST

Castlewigg, DG8 8DP, 2 miles from Whithorn. Land and barony acquired by Andrew, 5th Sheriff of Wigtownshire, in 1543. Only ruins remain, close to the site of a caravan park.

Cruggleton Castle, Garlieston, DG8 8HF. Once one of the most impregnable castles in Scotland and secured by the Agnews of Lochnaw during the 17th century. Now a ruin.

AGNEW ANCIENT

Dalreagle Farm, DG8 9BG, was another Agnew residence.

Innermessan Castle, DG9 8QP. Remains of 12th-century seat of Agnew chiefs until purchased by Earl of Stair in 1723.

Lochnaw Castle, Stranraer, DG9 0RN. Thirteenth-century castle ruin on island in loch. The later Lochnaw Castle, dating from the 15th century, is run as a guest house.

Lochryan House, Stranraer, DG9 8HP. Built for Captain James Agnew and acquired through marriage by the Wallace family.

Old Leswalt Kirkyard, DG9 0LW. Agnew Mausoleum. There is a memorial tower to Sir Andrew Agnew, 7th Baronet.

Scottish National Gallery, Edinburgh, EH2 2EL. On display is a splendid portrait of Lady Agnew of Lochnaw, wife of Sir Andrew Agnew, 9th Baronet, by John Singer Sargent.

# ARTHUR (MACARTHUR)

**Chief of the Name and Arms:** John MacArthur of that Ilk
**Motto:** 'By fidelity and work' ('*Fide et opera*')
**Crest:** Two laurel branches in orle proper (a fruited laurel wreath)
**Plant Badge:** Wild thyme
www.clanarthur.org

Mythology suggests that the 'Children of Arthur' descend from the legendary King Arthur of the Round Table, the ruler of the Strathclyde Britons who was allegedly born at Red Hall in Dumbarton in the 6th century. Closely connected with Clan Campbell, to the extent that the MacArthurs at one time held that Chiefship, this is one of Argyll's oldest clans. For their support of Robert the Bruce in the early 14th century, Clan Mhic Artair was granted extensive lands on Loch Awe. These were mostly confiscated from Clan MacDougall, who had opposed Bruce. At the height of the MacArthurs' influence, the chief was appointed Captain of Dunstaffnage Castle.

However, in the 15th century, Iain MacArthur of Strachur was executed by order of James I in his bid to purge the unruly Highland chiefs. The clan scattered, allowing MacCailean Mór and Clan Campbell to take over MacArthur lands.

The MacArthurs of Islay were armourers and blacksmiths to Clan Donald, and the MacArthurs of Skye were appointed hereditary pipers to the Lords of the Isles. They became hereditary keepers of the grave of Flora MacDonald, heroine of the 1745 Rising.

## ANCESTRAL INTEREST

Dunstaffnage Castle, Oban, PA37 1PZ. Partially ruined and
   guarding the seaward approach to the Firth of Lorn. Historic
   Environment Scotland.

McArthur's Head lighthouse on the Sound of Islay. Established
   1861.

The MacArthur Pipers cairn, Duntulm, Isle of Skye.

Tiricladdich (the shore land), Argyll, PA33 1AQ. Ancestral
   domain on Loch Awe.

# BARCLAY

**Chief of the Name and Arms**: Peter Barclay of Towie of that Ilk
**Motto**: 'Either action or death' ('*Aut agere aut mori*')
**Crest**: A hand holding a dagger
www.clanbarclayinternational.org

It is generally accepted that the Barclays accompanied William the Conqueror in his invasion of England in 1066. Representatives of the family moved to Scotland in 1069 with St Margaret Atheling when she married King Malcolm III, and settled in Aberdeenshire where John de Berchelei was rewarded with the lands of Towie.

Sir Walter de Berkeley served as Chamberlain of Scotland in 1171, and Sir David Barclay supported Robert the Bruce in the Wars of Scottish Independence. A branch of the family was established at Urie near Stonehaven in Kincardineshire, and Colonel David Barclay served in the army of King Gustavus Adolphus of Sweden.

Living in close proximity to the North Sea, the enterprising Barclays established shipping and trading ties with mainland Europe. In 1621, a letter of safe conduct was signed for Peter Barclay from Banff to settle in Rostock in Mecklenburg. One of his descendants was the Russian Field Marshal Prince Michael Barclay de Tolly who became Russia's Minister of War in 1810 and was given command of the Russian armies fighting against Napoleon. For his successful 'scorched earth' tactics, he was created a prince by the Tsar. His portrait hangs in the Hermitage Museum in St Petersburg.

**ANCESTRAL INTEREST**

Balvaird Castle, Cupar, KY14 7SR. The estate was acquired in 1495 by Sir Andrew Murray, son of Murray of Tullibardine (ancestor of the earls of Mansfield), through marriage to Margaret Barclay, daughter of James Barclay of Kippo. Historic Environment Scotland.

Towie Barclay Castle, Turriff, Aberdeenshire, AB53 8EP. Built in 1593 by Sir Alexander Barclay de Tolly. In the 1960s the abandoned castle was bought and restored by the musician Marc Ellington and it remains the private home of Ellington family.

# BORTHWICK

**Chief of the Name and Arms:**
John Hugh Borthwick of that Ilk, 24th Lord Borthwick
**Motto:** 'He who leads' (*Qui conducti*)
**Plant Badge:** A stem of two roses gules leaved,
barbed and seeded, vert
www.clanborthwick.com

Andreas Borthwick was among those who accompanied St Margaret, sister of Edgar the Atheling, claimant to the English throne, to Scotland in 1067, and is therefore thought by some historians to have been of Hungarian descent. However, the name Borthwick also has a territorial connection originating from the Borthwick Water in Roxburghshire.

Thomas de Borthwick held a charter for lands near Lauder in 1357. In 1378, William de Borthwick owned lands in Midlothian which became known as Borthwick. In 1425, the 1st Lord Borthwick was sent to England as a hostage for the return of James I to Scotland.

The Borthwicks were loyal supporters of the Royal House of Stewart/Stuart, fought for James IV at the Battle of Flodden in 1513 and for the Royalist cause during the Civil War. Borthwick Castle was besieged following the Battle of Dunbar in 1650. The direct chiefly line came to a halt following the death of the 9th Lord Borthwick in 1675, but was reinstated a century later when Henry Borthwick of Neathorn was recognised by the House of Lords as a direct descendant of the 1st Lord Borthwick. However, he died without issue and the title was thereafter much disputed by various branches of the family. In 1986, Major John Henry Borthwick of Crookston was finally recognised as 23rd Lord Borthwick by the Court of the Lord Lyon King of Arms.

BORTHWICK MODERN

**ANCESTRAL INTEREST**

Borthwick Castle, Middleton, Gorebridge, Midlothian
EH23 4QY. Built by the 1st Lord Borthwick in 1430. Mary,
Queen of Scots stayed here following her elopement with the
Earl of Bothwell in 1567. Currently run as a hospitality
destination.

Crookston, Heriot, EH38 5YS. Seat of the head of the Borthwick
family.

Newbyres Castle, Gorebridge, Midlothian, EH23 4TP. Not
much remains of this 16th-century tower house built by the
Borthwicks in the mid-17th century.

Ravenstone Castle, near Whithorn, Wigtownshire, DG8 8DS.
Owned by Lord Borthwick in the 19th century.

# BRODIE

**Chief of the Name and Arms:**
Alexander Brodie of Brodie, 27th Chief
**Motto:** 'Unite'
**Plant Badge:** Periwinkle
www.clanbrodie.us

The Brodies are an ancient Highland tribe of Pictish descent. Michael, Thane of Brodie, received a charter from Robert the Bruce confirming the Thanage of Brodie shortly before the Battle of Bannockburn in 1314. Alas, all of the clan records were destroyed when Brodie Castle was attacked and burned in 1645 by Lord Lewis Gordon during the Covenanter conflicts.

The Brodies were proactive in the north-east during the 15th and 16th centuries. Alexander Brodie of Brodie was denounced as a rebel in 1550 for attacking Alexander Cumming of Altyre. However, his son David had the Brodie lands erected into a free barony under charter of the Great Seal in 1597. In 1727, another Alexander Brodie of Brodie was appointed Lord Lyon King of Arms. He remained Lord Lyon during the Jacobite Rising of 1745 and attended on the Duke of Cumberland at the Battle of Culloden.

There are several distinguished branches of this clan, not least the Brodies of Lethen. Sir Benjamin Collins Brodie was surgeon to William IV and Queen Victoria. Deacon William Brodie who lived in Edinburgh was respectable by day and a thief by night. He was executed by a mechanism of his own devising in 1788.

## ANCESTRAL INTEREST

Brodie Castle, Forres, Moray, IV36 2TE. The first castle was
   erected in 1567 and was rebuilt after being destroyed in the
   mid-17th century during the Covenanter period. In the care
   of the National Trust for Scotland.

# BRUCE

**Chief of the Name and Arms:**
The Rt Honourable Earl of Elgin & Kincardine, KT
**Motto**: 'We have been' (*Fuimus*)
**Plant Badge**: Rosemary
www.familyofbruceinternational.org; www.brucefamily.com

Having accompanied William the Conqueror to England in 1066, the de Brus family from Brix, near Cherbourg in Normandy, was granted lands in Surrey and Yorkshire. In a later generation, Robert de Brus accompanied his friend David I to Scotland when he returned from England to be crowned in 1124 and he was given the lordship of Annandale in Dumfries and Galloway.

It was through the marriage of Robert, 4th Lord of Annandale, to Isobel of Huntingdon, granddaughter of King David and niece of King William the Lion, that the family acquired its claim to the Scottish throne to which Robert, 7th of Annandale, succeeded in 1306.

Although the name is dominated by the Royal line of King Robert, victor of Bannockburn, and his brother Edward, proclaimed High King of Ireland in 1315 (d.1318), the Bruces of Clackmannan (1334) and Kinloss (1608), and the earldoms of Elgin (1633) and Kincardine (1647) are descended from the same family.

The 7th Earl of Elgin became a diplomat and, between 1810 and 1812, rescued the Parthenon Stones (Elgin Marbles) from the Acropolis in Athens (then under Turkish rule). His son served as Governor General of Canada and Viceroy of India, a post also held by his son, the 9th Earl. Sir William Bruce (1630–1710) was architect for the restoration of the Palace of Holyroodhouse. Sir James Bruce (1730–94), son of David Bruce of Kinnaird,

BRUCE MODERN

travelled up the Nile to Ethiopia (formerly Abyssinia) to trace the source of the Blue Nile.

## ANCESTRAL INTEREST

Battle of Bannockburn Visitor Centre, Whins of Milton, Stirling, FK7 0LJ. An equestrian statue of Robert the Bruce by Pilkington Jackson stands nearby.

Broomhall House, Charlestown, Dunfermline, KY11 3DU. Ancestral seat of the earls of Elgin and Kincardine.

Lochmaben Castle, Lockerbie, DG11 1JE. Ancient stronghold of the Bruces of Annandale.

# BUCHANAN

**Chief:** John Michael Buchanan of that Ilk and Arnprior
**Motto:** 'Henceforth forward the honour shall grow ever brighter'
('*Clarior hinc honos*')
**Plant Badge:** Bilberry and oak
www.theclanbuchanan.com

A Stirlingshire clan of Pictish origin, the Buchanans traditionally held lands on the east side of Loch Lomond. They are thought to have descended from an Irishman called Anselan O'Kyan who settled in Lennox in the 11th century. In the 13th century, Gilbert, seneschal to the Earl of Lennox, obtained a portion of the lands of Buchanan and took his name from them. A charter from Alexander II in 1225 confirmed the ownership of an island in Loch Lomond which is now called Clairinch.

During the Wars of Scottish Independence, Clan Buchanan supported Robert the Bruce and aided his escape from the English in 1306. In 1421, Sir Alexander Buchanan led his clansmen in support of the French against the English at the Battle of Baugé. In the 15th century a feud broke out between the Buchanans and Clan MacLaren and, in 1497, Kenneth Mackenzie of Kintail, Chief of Clan Mackenzie, was killed by the Laird of Buchanan. The Buchanans fought against the English at the Battle of Flodden in 1513 where the Chief's eldest son, Patrick, was killed.

The principal line became extinct in 1762 and the clan lands were sold by John Buchanan, 22nd Chief, to the 3rd Marquis of Montrose. Thereafter, the clan dispersed. James Buchanan, an American lawyer of Ulster Scots descent, became 15th President of the United States of America. In 1753, the Buchanans legally incorporated the name, septs and branches of the clan and thus became the oldest established Scottish Clan Society in the world.

## ANCESTRAL INTEREST

Buchanan Castle, Drymen, Stirlingshire, G63 0HY. Today the
seat of Clan Graham although surrounding lands were held
by the Buchanans. The partly demolished castle sits on the
Buchanan Castle Golf Club.

Clairinch (the Flat Island), south-west of Balmaha on Loch
Lomond, is a National Nature Reserve.

# CAMERON

**Chief of the Name and Arms:**
Donald Cameron of Lochiel, 27th Chief
**Motto:** 'Let us unite' (*Aonaibh ri cheile*)
**Plant Badge**: Crowberry or Oak
www.clancameron.org.uk; www.clan-cameron.org;
www.clancameronmuseum.co.uk

Clan Cameron springs from a medieval tribal grouping of the MacMartins of Letterfinlay, the MacGillonies of Strone and the MacSorleys of Glen Nevis, all situated on the west side of Loch Lochy and the River Lochy in Lochaber. Collectively, their lands included Glen Loy and Loch Arkaig, Glen Kingie, Glen Dessary, Glen Pean and Glen Mallie, and the clan gave its allegiance to the Lordship of the Isles.

Donald Dubh, progenitor of the Lochiel Chiefs through marriage to the heiress of Letterfinlay, led the clan in support of Donald, Lord of the Isles, at the indecisive and extremely bloody Battle of Harlaw in 1411. This was fought close to Inverurie in Aberdeenshire over the possession of the earldom of Ross.

Camerons were staunch followers of the Royal House of Stuart, taking part in the Jacobite Rising of 1689. In 1715, the ageing Sir Ewen of Lochiel made over his estates to his grandson so that his son John could muster the clan on behalf of the Old Pretender, a gesture for which he was sent into exile. In 1745, John's son Donald, who came to be known as the 'Gentle Lochiel', was sufficiently won over by Bonnie Prince Charlie to also bring out the clan. The clan lands were later restored to the 22nd Chief in 1748.

The Camerons of Erracht (tartan displayed opposite) descend from a son of Lochiel in the 15th century.

CAMERON OF ERRACHT MODERN

## ANCESTRAL INTEREST

Achnacarry, Spean Bridge, PH34 4EJ. This remains the Clan Seat of Lochiel. The current house stands next to the site of the original castle which was burned by the Duke of Cumberland's soldiers in 1746. Private home.

Annat, north shore of Loch Eil in Lochaber. Ancient seat of the Camerons of Lochiel.

Kilmallie, Fort William, Lochaber. An obelisk commemorates Colonel John Cameron of Fassiefern.

Loch a' Chlaidheimh (the Loch of the Sword), near Rannoch Station, PH17 2QA. In the 17th century, Ewen, 17th Chief, met the Earl of Atholl on disputed ground. Gormsuil, a witch, forewarned Lochiel of treachery.

# CAMPBELL

**Chief of the Name and Arms:**
His Grace the 13th Duke of Argyll
**Motto:** 'Forget not' (*'Ne obliviscaris'*)
**Plant Badge:** Bog myrtle
www.ccsna.org

The Campbell name is derived from the Gaelic 'Cam-beul' meaning 'crooked mouth', and the Gaelic clan name is 'Clann na Duibhne', which derived from Diarmid O'Dhuibne of Lochawe. Sir Colin og Campbell of Lochawe was recognised by the King of Scots in 1292 as one of the principal Barons of Argyll.

Sir Colin's son Neil was a staunch supporter of Robert the Bruce and was rewarded with extensive grants of land. The Campbells of Strachur claim descent from Sir Colin's brother, and from a younger son came the Campbells of Loudon. From a younger son of Sir Neil come the Campbells of Inverawe.

The Campbells of Glenorchy (earls of Breadalbane) extended Campbell influence east until it embraced Loch Tay. Muriel, daughter of the 7th Thane of Cawdor, married Sir John Campbell, 3rd son of Argyll, in 1510. When she died, she settled the Thanedom on their grandson, hence the Campbell of Cawdor line.

As the power of the MacDonald Lords of the Isles declined, the Cambells benefited, acquiring Knapdale and Kintyre, Mull, Morvern, Coll and Tiree.

## ANCESTRAL INTEREST

Castle Campbell (Castle Glume), near Dollar, FK14 7PP.
Acquired by the Earl of Argyll in the 15th century. Cawdor Castle and Gardens, near Nairn, IV12 5RD. Seat of the earls of Cawdor and open to the public.

Finlarig Castle, near Killin, FK21 8TU. The original seat of the
    Campbells of Glenorchy.

Innis Chonnel, Loch Awe, Argyll. Island and remains of original
    castle built in the 11th century.

Inveraray Castle, Inveraray, PA32 8XE. Seat of the dukes of
    Argyll and headquarters of the Clan Campbell Societies.

Kilchurn Castle, Loch Awe, PA33 1AF. Built by Campbell of
    Glenorchy in 1440.

Loudoun Castle, Ayr, KA7 1HR. Built in the 16th century and
    acquired by Campbells of Loudoun.

Taymouth Castle, Kenmore, PH15 2EZ. Built for Sir Colin
    Campbell of Glenorchy in 1580 and former home to the earls
    and marquesses of Breadalbane.

# CARMICHAEL

**Chief of the Name and Arms:**
Richard Carmichael of Carmichael
**Motto:** 'Always ready' (*Tout jour prest*)
www.carmichael.co.uk

The Carmichael family originate from the lands of Carmichael in Lanarkshire from which they take their name. Their lands were originally a part of Douglasdale granted to Clan Douglas by Robert the Bruce in 1321. Around 1375, Sir John de Carmichael was given a charter of the lands of Carmichael by William, Earl of Douglas. The Barony of Carmichael was confirmed on the family in 1414.

Sir John de Carmichael of Meadowflat (later Carmichael) fought in France with the Scottish army sent to assist the French against English invasion. In 1421 at the Battle of Baugé he fought a duel with the Duke of Clarence, brother of Henry V of England, and knocked him off his horse, breaking a spear. Catherine, Sir John's daughter, became the mistress of James V and bore him a son, half-brother to Mary, Queen of Scots.

Sir James Carmichael, 1st Lord Carmichael, supported the Royalist cause but his son chose to follow the Parliamentarians and commanded the Clydesdale Regiment at Marston Moor in 1644 and at Philiphaugh in 1645. He was raised to the peerage in 1647 and his grandson was created Earl of Hyndford in 1701.

**ANCESTRAL INTEREST**

Carmichael Visitor Centre and Farm Shop, Warrenhill Road, Thankerton, ML12 6PF.

Mauldslie Castle, Lanarkshire, ML8 5QE. Built for the 5th Earl of Hyndford by Robert Adam in 1792 and demolished in 1935.

# CARNEGIE

**Chief of the Name and Arms:** His Grace the 4th Duke of Fife
**Motto:** 'Dread God'

The name derives from the lands of 'Carryneggy' (Carnegie) in Angus, confirmed upon John de Balinhard by David II in 1358. The direct line of the Carnegies of that line came to an end in 1563 and from Duthac de Carnegie, second son of John, derives the House of Southesk.

Sir David Carnegie was created Earl of Southesk by Charles I in 1633 and, although the title and estates were forfeited after the Carnegies supported the Old Pretender in 1715, they were later recovered. The Earldom of Northesk was assumed in 1662 by John, younger brother of the 1st Earl of Southesk, previously Earl of Ethie. The 7th Earl of Northesk was third in command of the Mediterranean Fleet commanded by Vice-Admiral Lord Nelson at the Battle of Trafalgar in 1805. The 11th Earl of Southesk married HRH Princess Maud, daughter of the Princess Royal and a granddaughter of Edward VII. Her son, as well as being heir to the earldom of Southesk, and Chief of Clan Carnegie, inherited the Fife dukedom in 1959.

A famous descendant, born the son of a weaver in Dunfermline in 1835, was the steel tycoon Andrew Carnegie who, having amassed a fortune in the USA, became one of the richest men in the world.

## ANCESTRAL INTEREST

Elsick House, Stonehaven, AB39 3NT. Home of the Duke of Fife. (Private, but can also be hired as a wedding venue.)
Ethie Castle, Inverkeilor, DD11 5SP. Purchased by the Carnegie family in 1665.

CARNEGIE ANCIENT

Farnell Castle, Brechin, DD9 6UH. Former residence of the
 Bishops of Brechin, acquired by the Southesk family in 1632.
Kinnaird Castle, Brechin, DD9 6TZ. Built for the Carnegie
 family who acquired the lands here in the 15th century. The
 castle was rebuilt in the 19th century and enlarged.
Skibo Castle, Dornoch, IV25 3RQ. Purchased by Andrew
 Carnegie as his family home in 1898 and now houses the
 Carnegie Club, a prestigious private members club.

# CHISHOLM

**Chief of the Name and Arms:**
Andrew Francis Chisholm of that Ilk
**Motto**: 'I am fierce with the fierce' (*Feros ferio*)
**Plant Badge**: Fern
www.clanchisholmsociety.org

Originally spelled De Chesholme, this family originates in Roxburghshire. The Highland and Lowland Chisholms descend from a common ancestor. One of the family married Margaret, Lady of Erchless, daughter and heiress to Wyland of the Aird, and became Constable of Urquhart Castle on Loch Ness. His son Thomas, born in 1473, succeeded to his maternal grandfather's lands in Morayshire and is the ancestor of the Chisholms of Comar and Strathglass. Branches of the Highland clan are Kinneries and Lierty, Knockfin and Mackerach.

From the Borders family sprang the Chisholms of Cromlix in Perthshire, three of whom served as successive Archbishops of Dunblane. The Chisholms supported Prince Charles Edward Stuart in the 1745 Jacobite Rising (although two of the Chisholm sons fought with the Government troops). After his defeat at Culloden, the Prince took refuge in Strathglass and and among those who aided him in his escape were followers of the Chisholm clan.

The Highland Clearances of the 18th and 19th centuries dispersed large numbers of the Chisholm clan overseas to Nova Scotia, where they generally prospered.

34

## ANCESTRAL INTEREST

Erchless Castle, Strathglass, IV4 7JU. Originally built for the
   Bissetts, this passed to the Chisholms in the 15th century
   through marriage to Margaret, Lady of Erchless. The castle
   was owned by the Chisholm family until 1935. Now privately
   owned.

Urquhart Castle, Drumnadrochit, IV63 6XJ. In the 14th century,
   Robert de Chisholm, founder of the northern line of the
   Chisholm clan, married the daughter of the Constable of
   Urquhart Castle and in turn became Constable himself.

# COCHRANE

**Chief of the Name and Arms:** The Rt Hon. Ian Alexander
Douglas Blair Cochrane, Earl of Dundonald
**Motto:** 'By valour and exertion' (*Virtute et labore*)
**Plant Badge:** Sea Holly
www.clancochrane.org

There is a tradition that the Cochranes descend
from a Viking invader who settled in Renfrewshire
between the 8th and 10th centuries. However, it
can definitely be confirmed that the Cochranes
were well established in that area when William,
Lord Cochrane, purchased the Lordship and
Barony of Paisley from the Earl of Angus in 1653.

The Dundonald estate and its castle came into the hands of
the family around 1638. In 1669, Sir William Cochrane, Baron
Cochrane, was created Earl of Dundonald for supporting the
Royalist cause during the Wars of the Three Kingdoms.

Archibald, 9th Earl of Dundonald, was a scientist and
inventor. Thomas, 10th Earl, served with great distinction in the
Royal Navy and over the 19th century commanded the Chilean,
Peruvian, Brazilian and Greek navies. In 1824 he was created
Marquess of Maranhão in Brazil.

COCHRANE MODERN

## ANCESTRAL INTEREST

Auchindoun Castle, Keith, AB55 4DR. Allegedly built by
Thomas Cochrane, a favourite of James III, but passed to the
Gordons in 1567. Largely destroyed in 1571 during a feud
between the Gordons and Clan Mackintosh.

Dundonald Castle and Visitor Centre, Kilmarnock, KA2 9HD.
Historic home of Robert II of Scotland and his son Robert
III. Bought by Sir William Cochrane in 1638 and gifted to
the State by his descendant, the 13th Earl of Dundonald, in
1953.

Lochnell Castle, Benderloch, Argyll, PA37 1QT. Purchased by the
Cochrane family in 1912, sold and then repurchased in 1962.
Family home.

# COLQUHOUN

**Chief:** Sir Malcolm Colquhoun of Luss Bt
**Motto:** 'If I can' ('*Si je puis*')
**Plant Badge:** Hazel saplings
www.clancolquhoun.com

This is a territorial name taken from the Barony of Colquhoun in Dunbartonshire. The founder of the family was Humphrey de Kilpatrick or Kirkpatrick, who obtained a grant of lands in the reign of Alexander II. The lands of Luss were acquired in the 14th century through marriage to the 'Fair Maid of Luss', a descendant of Maldwin, Dean of the Lennox.

In 1603, during the Chiefship of Alexander Colquhoun, 17th of Luss, Clan Gregor attacked Luss. At the Battle of Glen Fruin, the 'Glen of Sorrow', a further massacre took place. Clan Gregor was outlawed by James VI and the MacGregor Chief was caught through Campbell intrigue and hanged with eleven of his principal clansmen.

Sir John Colquhoun of Luss was a necromancer and the last known to openly promote witchcraft in Scotland. He became one of the first Nova Scotia baronets and married the Marquis of Montrose's sister, subsequently eloping with another of Montrose's sisters.

John Caldwell Calhoun (1782–1850) was Vice President of the United States of America. A Lieutenant Jimmy Calhoun of the 7th US Cavalry fell fighting the Sioux tribe at Custer's Last Stand at the Battle of the Little Bighorn.

COLQUHOUN ANCIENT

## ANCESTRAL INTEREST

Dumbarton Castle, Dumbarton, G82 1JJ. Sir John Colquhoun
of Luss was Governor under James II.

Glen Fruin, Loch Lomond & Trossachs National Park. Tragic
defeat of Alexander, 12th Laird of Luss, with 200
Colquhouns by MacGregors in 1603.

Inchmurrin, Loch Lomond, G63 0JY. Ruined castle where
Sir John Colquhoun was murdered with his attendants.

Luss Estates, G83 8RH. Held by the Colquhouns since the
14th century.

Rossdhu, Luss, G83 8NT. Ancestral seat of Colquhoun Chiefs.
Now site of the Loch Lomond Golf Club.

# COMYN/CUMMING

**Chief of the Name and Arms:**
Sir Alexander 'Alastair' Penrose Cumming of Altyre
**Motto**: 'Courage'
**Plant Badge**: Common sallow (pussy willow)
www.clancumming.us

In the reign of Alexander III, the Comyn family from Normandy held the earldoms of Atholl, Buchan and Menteith. Descended from Richard Comyn who served as Chancellor to David I, the Comyns/Cummings became immensely powerful in medieval Scotland. Through marriage to the sister of King John Balliol, and his descent from King Duncan, John de Comyn, Lord of Badenoch, also known as the 'Red Comyn', had a strong claim to the Scottish throne when it fell vacant on the death of four-year-old Princess Margaret of Norway who died in 1290 on her way to Scotland to be crowned Queen. Following a confrontation with Robert the Bruce in Dumfries in 1306, where the Red Comyn was killed, the clan went into decline. After Bruce's victory at Bannockburn, Comyn lands in the north were largely confiscated and divided up among Bruce's supporters.

Feuds with Clan Macpherson, Clan Mackintosh, Clan Shaw and Clan Brodie continued throughout the 15th and 16th centuries, with the Cummings of Altyre acquiring the Chiefly role. During the 17th century, Clan Comyn members served as Hereditary Pipers to Clan Grant.

Several families of Comyns/Cummings emigrated to North America, Australia, South Africa and New Zealand in the 18th and 19th centuries. Others settled in Mauritius and La Réunion in the Indian Ocean.

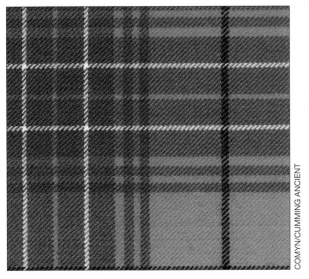

## ANCESTRAL INTEREST

Altyre Estate, Forres, IV36 2SH. Seat of Cumming Clan Chief.

Blair Castle, Blair Atholl, PH18 5TL. Originally occupied by the Comyns; their tower remains.

Comyns Castle, East Kilbride, G74 5BY. Acquired by David Comyn through marriage in the 13th century.

Dunphail Castle, Forres, IV36 2QQ. Headless ghosts are said to inhabit the ruins.

Inverlochy Castle, Fort William, PH33 6TF. Original castle is ruined but Comyn's Tower can still be seen.

Lochindorb, PH26 3PY. A formidable island stronghold in the middle of Badenoch held by the Wolf of Badenoch.

41

# DRUMMOND

**Chief of the Name and Arms:** The 9th Earl of Perth
**Motto:** 'Honour crowns virtue' (*Virtutem coronat honos*')
**Plant Badge:** Wild thyme and holly

The surname derives from the lands of Drummond or Drymen in Stirlingshire. Malcolm Beg, Steward of the Earldom of Strathearn in 1255, is the first on record and his son, Sir Malcolm, took the name Drummond. Margaret Drummond married David II in 1364 and her niece Anabella Drummond was the wife of Robert III.

The Drummond Barony was created in 1488, and the 4th Lord was created Earl of Perth in 1605. The younger brother of the 3rd Lord Drummond was created Lord Maderty by James VI in 1609 and from him descend the Viscounts Strathallan.

The Drummonds supported the House of Stuart and followed the fortunes of James VII who created them dukes of Perth and Melfort. James, 3rd Duke of Perth, was a Lieutenant General of the Jacobite army. The Drummond estates passed through an heiress to the earls of Ancaster. In 1853, George Drummond, Duc de Melfort in the French peerage, was restored to the title of Earl of Perth by an Act of the UK parliament.

DRUMMOND OF PERTH MODERN

## ANCESTRAL INTEREST

Drummond Castle, Muthill, Crieff, PH7 4HN. Built in 1491, it
was sacked by the army of Oliver Cromwell in the Wars of
the Three Kingdoms. Modern house was begun in 1689 and
passed to the Willoughby de Eresby, earls of Ancaster.
Gardens are open to the public.

Megginch Castle, Errol, Perth, PH2 7SW. Clan Drummond seat
from 15th century. Private home although gardens open
under Scotland's Gardens Scheme.

Stobhall, Perth, PH2 6DR. Fourteenth-century seat of the earls
of Perth. New owners.

# DUNBAR

**Chief of the Name and Arms:** Sir James Michael Dunbar
**Motto:** 'In readiness' (*In promptu*)
www.clandunbar.com

Crinan the Thane and Seneschal of the Isles was father to King Duncan I and of Maldred, whose son Gospatric became Earl of Northumbria in 1067. In 1072, he was deprived of that earldom by William the Conqueror and fled to Scotland where Malcolm III gifted him the earldom of Dunbar.

Gospatric's descendant, Patrick, 8th Earl of Dunbar, also became Earl of March, and his son married Agnes, daughter of Thomas Randolph, 1st Earl of Moray, and on the death of her brother she inherited the Moray title. On her death the Dunbar earldom devolved to her nephew who was created Earl of Moray in 1372 and married Princess Marjorie, daughter of Robert II.

The Dunbars of Caithness who appear in the 15th century descend from the Dunbars of Westfield. Two Westfield sons married the co-heiresses of Dunbar of Mochrum and of Cumnock, and eventually there were six baronetcies in the family: Baldoon and Mochrum in Wigtownshire; Durn in Banffshire; Hempriggs in Caithness; Boath in Nairn and Northfield in Morayshire. The poet William Dunbar (*c.*1460–*c.*1520) was born in East Lothian.

44

## ANCESTRAL INTEREST

Dunbar Castle, Dunbar, EH42 1EY. Picturesque ruin of 14th-century fortification defended by 'Black Agnes' Dunbar against the English in 1338.

Elgin Cathedral, Elgin, IV30 1HU. Scene of 'Bloody Vespers', a murderous fight between the Dunbar and Innes families in 1555.

Mochrum, Dumfries and Galloway. Once owned by the Dunbar clan.

# DURIE

**Chief of the Name and Arms:** Andrew Durie of Durie
**Motto:** 'I trust' ('*Confido*')
www.brucedurie.co.uk

It is generally accepted that the Duries first arrived in Scotland in the retinue of St Margaret in 1069 and, following her marriage to Malcolm III, settled in the Kingdom of Fife where their names appear in various important charters over the 14th and 15th centuries. The stone of a house built in 1520 at Craigluscar, near Leven, carries a shield carrying the Durie Arms and initials of George Durie and his wife, Margaret Bruce. Craigluscar remained under Durie ownership until the early 20th century.

Abbot George Durie was Commendator and last Abbot of Dunfermline (1530–61). A staunch supporter of Mary, Queen of Scots, he fled to France, taking with him the relics of St Margaret for safekeeping to the Scots College in Paris. A Jesuit Durie in France was later implicated in the plot to depose Elizabeth I of England. Several Durie properties in Fife were confiscated by the Crown at the time of the Reformation.

Thereafter, Clan Durie remained chiefless until 1988 when Lt Colonel Raymond Durie of Durie was confirmed from his grandmother Elizabeth Durie of Craigluscar's descent from Abbot George.

DURIE

**ANCESTRAL INTEREST**

Dunfermline Abbey, Fife, KY12 7PE.

Rossend Castle, Burntisland, KY3 0DF. Built in 1382 and has an
  armorial tablet above the entrance bearing the Durie Arms
  and the date 1544.

# ELLIOT(T)

**Chief of the Name and Arms:**
Madam Margaret Elliott of Redheugh
**Motto:** 'Boldly and rightly' (*Fortiter et recte*')
**Plant Badge:** White hawthorn
www.elliotclan.com

A family of southern Scotland, one of the great 'Riding Clans' of the Scottish Borders. The Ellots of Redheugh (the 'i' was introduced into the name in the mid-17th century) are recognised as the principal family. One fell at the Battle of Flodden in 1513, and another was appointed Captain of Hermitage Castle. When James VI set about curtailing the lawless Border clans, a number of Elotts scattered, some to Ulster. The lands of the Ellots of Redheugh were passed on to the Elliots of Stobs, who took over the Chiefship.

Gilbert Elliot, from a branch of the Stobs family, received a knighthood, then baronetcy, having served as a Lord of Session under the courtesy title of Lord Minto. The 3rd Baronet became Lord of the Admiralty and Keeper of the Signet in Scotland, and the 4th Baronet was appointed Viceroy of Corsica and Governor General of Bengal in India (1807–13). He was created 1st Earl of Minto.

The 4th Earl of Minto was appointed Governor General of Canada (1898–1904) and Viceroy and Governor General of Canada (1905–10).

ELLIOT MODERN

## ANCESTRAL INTEREST

Fatlips Castle, Denholm, TD9 8SH. Peel tower and former seat
of the Turnbull family, but was restored in 1857 by Sir
Gilbert Elliot who employed the architect Robert Lorimer to
renovate the interiors.

Hermitage Castle, Hawick, TD9 0LU. Several Elliots served as
captain of this fortress dating from c.1240. Historic
Environment Scotland.

Redheugh, Newcastleton, TD9 0SB. Seat of Elliott Chief. Private
home.

Stobs Castle, Hawick, TD9 9SF. Former seat of chief. Private
home.

# ERSKINE

**Chief: Chief of the Name and Arms:** James Thorne Erskine,
14th Earl of Mar and 16th Earl of Kellie
**Motto:** 'I think more' (*Je pense plus*)

The name of Erskine derives from the Barony of
Erskine in Renfrewshire which was held by Henry
de Erskine in the reign of Alexander II. Sir
Thomas de Erskine married Janet Keith,
granddaughter of Lady Eline de Mar, and their
son Robert became heir to one of the oldest Celtic
earldoms and Chief of the ancient 'Tribe of Mar'.

A Mormaer (earl) of Mar fought at the Battle of Clontarf in
1014. Gratney of Mar married Christian, sister of Robert the
Bruce, and their son Donald was Regent of Scotland. Donald's
son Thomas was Great Chamberlain of Scotland. In 1457, before
an Assize of Error, the earldom of Mar was found to have
devolved upon the Crown. Robert, 4th Lord Erskine, was killed
at the Battle of Flodden in 1513.

In 1565, John, 6th Lord Erskine, was restored as Earl of Mar
by Mary, Queen of Scots who, it seems, created a second
earldom of Mar, causing much confusion in centuries to come.
The ancient earldom of Mar is considered the premier earldom
of Scotland. The second earldom, created through marriage in
1565, acquired the earldom of Kellie in 1835 and the holder of
these titles is recognised as Chief of Clan Erskine. In 1715, John
Erskine, 6th Earl of Mar, led the Jacobite uprising. He was
attainted and his estates were forfeit to the Crown. They were
later repurchased by his brother James, Lord Grange, and David
Erskine of Dun.

**ANCESTRAL INTEREST**

Alloa Tower, Clackmannan, FK10 1PP. Fourteenth-century.

Cambo House, Kingsbarns, KY16 8QD. Seat of the Erskines of
   Cambo.
Dirleton Castle, East Lothian, EH39 5ER. Owned by Sir John
   Erskine of Gogar in the 17th century. Historic Environment
   Scotland.
Kellie Castle, Pittenweem, KY10 2RE. Acquired by Thomas
   Erskine in 1613. He became 1st Earl of Kellie and slew the
   Earl of Ruthven in the Gowrie Conspiracy against James VI.
   National Trust for Scotland; Braemar Castle, Braemar,
   AB35 5XR. Built by John, Earl of Mar (1562–1634).
Mar's Wark, Stirling, FK8 1EG. Remains of a townhouse
   occupied by the Regent Mar in 1670.

# FARQUHARSON

**Chief of the Name and Arms:** Philip Farquharson of Invercauld
**Motto:** 'By faith and fortitude' (*Fide et fortitudine*)
**Plant Badge:** Scots fir

Farquhar, son of Alexander Ciar, 3rd Shaw of Rothiemurchus, was the originator of this clan and came to Braemar before the end of the 14th century. Donald, 4th Chief, married Isabella Stewart, heiress of Invercauld, and he was appointed Keeper of the King's forests of Braemar. Farquhar's son, Finlay Mor, 1st Farquharson of Invercauld, was killed at the Battle of Pinkie in 1547.

From Donald there descended a number of Farquharson cadet families: Inverey, Finzean Monaltrie and Balmoral. Many of the Farquharsons fought for the Jacobite cause both within and outside the Clan Chattan confederation. Inverey supported the Old Pretender and Invercauld joined Prince Charles Edward Stuart at Perth, although he later went over to the Hanoverian government, claiming that he had been forced to support the Prince by his neighbour and feudal superior, the Earl of Mar.

Anne, Invercauld's daughter and wife of the Chief of Clan Mackintosh, restored the clan's honour when she contrived to scatter the English troops with a few of her father's men and thus enabled Prince Charles Edward Stuart to escape.

Henry Farquharson, who died in the 18th century, was founder of the School of Navigation in Moscow, Russia.

FARQUHARSON MODERN

## ANCESTRAL INTEREST

Braemar Castle, Braemar, AB35 5XR. Built by the Earl of Mar in
1628 and passed to the Farquharson family in 1732.

Cairn na Cumline (Cairn of Remembrance), two miles south-
west of Balmoral. Rallying ground of Clan Farquharson.

Invercauld House, Braemar, AB35 5TW. Private home.

# FERGUSSON

**Chief of the Name and Arms:**
Sir Charles Fergusson of Kilkerran Bt
**Motto:** 'Sweeter after difficulties' (*Dulcius ex asperis*)
**Plant Badge:** Little sunflower
www.cfsna.net

The first settlement of this clan seems to have been at Kintyre. Kilkerran, the seat of the Fergusson Chiefs in Ayrshire, is the modern Gaelic form of the name which derived from St Ciaran, one of the twelve apostles of Ireland who landed nearby at Dalruadhain in the 6th century.

The Fergussons of Kilkerran descend from Fergus, son of Fergus, in the time of Robert the Bruce. Fergus, King of Galloway, in the reign of David I, married a daughter of Henry I of England. The Fergussons of Craigdarroch in Dumfriesshire have a recorded history that dates back to a charter from David II in the 14th century. The Fergusson Chiefs allied themselves with the Kennedy earls of Cassillis in their feud against the Kennedy Lairds of Bargany.

Other branches of the family appear in Atholl. Their chief was Fergusson of Dunfallandy, and this family can be traced back to the 15th century.

The poet Robert Fergusson, who was so much admired by his near contemporary Robert Burns, presented a copy of his book of verses to his Kilkerran Chief. One of the most distinguished soldiers of the 20th century was Sir Bernard Fergusson, 1st Lord Ballantrae, who served as Governor-General of New Zealand from 1962 to 1967.

FERGUSON MODERN

## ANCESTRAL INTEREST

Kilkerran House, Maybole, KA19 7SE. Seat of Fergusson Chief.
Private residence.
Soulseat Abbey, Galloway. Founded for Premonstratensian
monks by Fergus of Galloway. Only a mound remains.

# FORBES

**Chief of the Name and Arms:** Malcolm, 23rd Lord Forbes
**Motto:** 'Grace me guide'
**Plant Badge:** Broom
www.clan-forbes.org

The Clan Forbes is said to originate from Ochonachur, who slew a bear and won the until-then uninhabitable Braes o' Forbes in Aberdeenshire. His family settled there, and in 1271 received a grant of lands from Alexander III.

Alexander de Forbes was one of the fiercest opponents of Edward I of England and lost his life defending Castle Urquhart on Loch Ness when it was attacked in 1296. The first Lord Forbes, created a baron in 1445, married a granddaughter of Robert II. There were a large number of Forbes cadet branches: Pitsligo, Boyndlie, Callendar, Castleton, Rothiemay, Colquhonny, Culloden, Tolquhon, Waterton, Thainstone, Pitnacalder, Foveran, Brux, Ledmacoy, Belnabodach, Kildrummy, Towie, Invernan, Ballinluig, Monymusk, Leslie, Corse, Craigievar and Echt.

Duncan Forbes of Culloden was Lord President of the Court of Session at the time of the 1745 Rising. Although he used his great influence to oppose the Jacobite cause, he afterwards fought to ease the cruel repercussions inflicted upon the Highlands.

## ANCESTRAL INTEREST

Castle Forbes, Alford, AB33 8DT. Nineteenth-century seat of Lord Forbes. Private home.

Corgarff Castle, Strathdon, AB36 8YP. During the feud between the Gordons and the Forbes family, Corgarff was defended by the wife of the absent Alexander Forbes. She and her

FORBES ANCIENT

children perished in the fire. The castle was rebuilt as a government barracks in the 18th century. Historic Environment Scotland.

Craigievar Castle, Alford, AB33 8JF. Built in 1626 for a Forbes laird, 'Danzig Willy', a prosperous merchant. National Trust for Scotland.

Culloden House, Inverness, IV2 7BZ. Once the home of Duncan Forbes, Laird of Culloden. Now a hotel.

Pitsligo Castle, Fraserburgh, AB43 7JJ. Built by Sir William Forbes. Ruins date from 1424.

# FORSYTH

**Chief of the Name and Arms:** Alistair Forsyth of that Ilk
**Motto:** 'A repairer of ruin' (*'Instaurator ruinae'*)
www.clanforsythsociety.net

There is an unsubstantiated tradition that the Forsyth family originated in Normandy and, having followed Eleanor of Provence to England when she married Henry II, moved to Northumberland and then to the Scottish Borders. Sadly the old records disappeared during the invasion of Oliver Cromwell in 1650.

However, it is on record that although William de Firsith was a signatory of the Ragman Roll in 1296, the family later supported Robert the Bruce with Osbert de Forsyth leading the clan at the Battle of Bannockburn in 1314. For this, he was confirmed in the lands of Sauchie in Stirlingshire.

A branch of the family moved to St Andrews and acquired the Barony of Nydie. Alexander, who became Sheriff Depute of Fife, died at the Battle of Flodden in 1513. His descendants acquired land in the vicinity of Falkland Palace and John Forsyth was appointed Falkland Pursuivant in 1538.

The Forsyth Family Association was founded in 1915, but it was not until 1977 that the Clan Forsyth Society was formed. In 1980, Alistair William Forsyth, who descended from a Falkland laird living in 1607, was recognised by the Lord Lyon King of Arms, supported by a petition representing 2,000 Forsyths.

FORSYTH MODERN

## ANCESTRAL INTEREST

Castle Dykes, Roberton. Only ruins remain.

Ethie Castle, Arbroath, DD11 5SP. Built c.1300 and home to
   Cardinal Beaton in the 16th century. The castle was restored
   by Alistair Forsyth of that Ilk and now serves as the clan's
   seat. Privately owned.

Falkland Palace, Cupar, KY15 7BY.

Stirling Castle, Stirling, FK8 1EJ. Forsyths served as Constables.

# FRASER

**Chief of the Name and Arms:** The Rt Hon. Lady Saltoun
**Motto:** 'All my hope is in God'
**Plant Badge:** Yew

Clan Fraser is considered to be a Scottish Lowland clan, as opposed to the Highland Clan Fraser of Lovat. Although both have a common ancestry, each has its own chief.

The worldwide family of Fraser traces its ancestry to Normandy. There is evidence to suggest that they sailed to England with William the Conqueror in 1066. The main line of Fraser in Scotland developed from Sir Gilbert of Touchfraser who died in 1263. Sir Lawrence Abernethy was created 1st Lord Saltoun in 1445 and, after several generations, the title and chiefship passed through the female line to Alexander Fraser of Philorth, son of Margaret Abernethy.

Alexander Fraser, 7th of Philorth, completed Fraserburgh Harbour in 1592. Sir Alexander, 8th of Philorth, acquired charters from James VI to create a burgh out of the fishing villages of Faithlie and Broadsea. He also intended to create a university, but his finances became so stretched that he had to dispose of the manor of Philorth. It was recovered by the family in 1661.

FRASER RED ANCIENT

## ANCESTRAL INTEREST

Cairnbulg Castle, Aberdeenshire, AB43 8UA. Seat of Clan Fraser. Originally known as Philorth Castle and one of 'the nine castles of the Knuckle', the rocky headland in north-east Aberdeenshire. Private estate.

Castle Fraser, Sauchen, Inverurie, AB51 7LD. One of the grandest Castles of Mar, begun in 1575 for the Frasers of Muchalls. National Trust for Scotland.

Pitsligo Castle, Rosehearty, Aberdeenshire, AB43 7JJ. A gift of marriage between the Fraser and Forbes families. Built 1424 and now a ruin.

# FRASER OF LOVAT

**Chief of the Name and Arms:** Simon Christopher Joseph
Fraser, 16th Lord Lovat and 5th Baron Lovat
**Motto:** 'I am ready' (*Je suis prest*)
**Plant Badge:** Strawberry
www.clanfraser.org

Sir Alexander Fraser of Philorth's younger brother
Simon, who fought for Robert the Bruce, is
believed to be the forebear of the branch of the
clan which acquired the Lordship of Lovat
through marriage to the daughter of the Earl of
Orkney and Caithness. From him the Chief of
the Clan Fraser of Lovat is called *MacShimidh*,
which means 'Son of Simon'. In 1815, the direct Lovat line failed
and Fraser of Strichen, a cadet of the Lovat family, was
recognised as chief.

Hugh Fraser, one of the hostages in England for the ransom
of James I, was created Baron of Kinnell but is better known as
first Lord Lovat. Simon, the 11th Lord Lovat, was outlawed in
1698 for having kidnapped the widow of the 9th Lord. He
returned from exile in 1715 to support the Hanoverian forces
against the Old Pretender and his outlawry was reversed.
However, in 1740, he joined the cause of Prince Charles Edward
Stuart who created him General of the Highlands and Duke of
Fraser. After the Battle of Culloden, he was taken prisoner by the
British Government and beheaded on Tower Hill in London in
1747. His honours and estate were forfeited but his son obtained
a full pardon, subsequently serving as a general in the British
Army.

The 15th Lord Lovat distinguished himself on the beaches of
Normandy with his Lovat Scouts during the Second World War.

FRASER OF LOVAT MODERN

## ANCESTRAL INTEREST

Beaufort Castle (previously Castle Dounie), Beauly, Inverness,
IV4 7GL. Built in 1880 and incorporating earlier buildings
dating from the 12th century. Traditional ancestral seat of the
Frasers of Lovat but sold by 15th Lord Lovat to meet
inheritance taxes.

# GORDON

**Chief of the Name and Arms:** The Most Honourable Granville
Gordon, 13th Marquess of Huntly
**Motto:** 'Bydand' ('Abiding steadfast')
**Plant Badge:** Rock ivy

 Established in the 12th century as the House of
Gordon, the surname is taken from the parish of
Gordon in Berwickshire. Adam de Gordon was
an Anglo-Norman and fought alongside King
Louis XI of France in the Crusades of 1270. A
supporter of Robert the Bruce, Sir Adam, Lord of
Gordon, was granted the Lordship of Strathbogie
in Banffshire. He died at the Battle of Halidon Hill in 1333.

Also supporting the Scottish monarchy, Sir Adam's great-
grandson died at the Battle of Homildon in 1402, leaving a
daughter and heiress Elizabeth who married Sir Alexander Seton,
second son of Sir William Seton of Seton. Their son was created
Earl of Huntly in 1449. For the following century, the Gordons
held autocratic sway over the Highlands and James VI was a
frequent guest at Huntly Castle, which until 1544 was known as
Strathbogie Castle. The 4th Earl had aspirations to marry Mary,
Queen of Scots and through a series of misunderstandings began
a rebellion which ended Gordon power after the clan's defeat at
the Battle of Corrichie in 1562.

The 6th Earl of Huntly took up arms against James VI in
1594. However, he somehow made peace with his monarch and
was rewarded by being created Marquis of Huntly. A dukedom
was created in 1684 but died with the 5th Duke in 1836.
However, his nearest heir was recognised as Chief of the Name.

The Gordons of Haddo, created earls of Aberdeen in 1682,
descend from Patrick Gordon of Methlic. George Hamilton-
Gordon, the 4th Earl, served as British Prime Minister from
1852–1855.

## ANCESTRAL INTEREST

Aboyne Castle, Aberdeenshire, AB34 5JP. Originally a motte-and-bailey castle built for the Bissets in the 13th century. Brought to the Gordons through marriage in 1449. It was restored by the Marquess of Huntly in the 20th century. Family home.

Gordon Castle, Fochabers, IV32 7PQ. Seat of the dukes of Richmond and Gordon.

Haddo House, Ellon, Aberdeenshire, AB41 7EQ. Seat of the marquesses of Aberdeen and Temair. National Trust for Scotland.

Huntly Castle, Aberdeenshire, AB54 4SH. Previously known as Strathbogie Castle, the surviving remains are impressive, Historic Environment Scotland.

# GRAHAM

**Chief of the Name and Arms:**
The Most Noble Graham 8th Duke of Montrose
**Motto:** 'Forget not' (*Ne oublie*)
**Plant Badge:** Laurel
www.clangrahamsociety.org

The first recorded Graham appears to be William de Graham, alive in the 12th century, although there is a legend that 'Gramus', who demolished the wall of defence built by the Roman Emperor Antoninus, is the earliest known ancestor.

King David I gifted William de Graham the lands of Abercorn and Dalkeith, and his descendants later acquired the lordships of Kinnaber and Old Montrose in 1325. Sir William Graham married Mary, second daughter of Robert III, and Patrick, their eldest grandson, was created Lord Graham, then Earl of Montrose in 1504. James, 5th Earl of Montrose, was the celebrated 1st Marquess of Montrose who was executed in 1650. The 4th Marquess was created Duke of Montrose for services to the Act of Union in 1707.

Another member of the clan was John Graham of Claverhouse, Viscount Dundee, the 'Bonnie Dundee' of legend, persecutor of the Covenanters and staunch supporter of the Jacobite cause who died at the Battle of Killiecrankie in 1689.

GRAHAM OF MENTEITH ANCIENT

## ANCESTRAL INTEREST

Braco Castle, Dunblane, FK15 9LA. Seat of the Graham family
in the 17th century.

Brodick Castle, Isle of Arran, KA27 8HY. Passed to the Montrose
family through marriage with daughter of 12th Duke of
Hamilton. National Trust for Scotland.

Buchanan Castle, Drymen, G63 0HY. Built for the 4th Duke of
Montrose between 1852–58, this remained home to the
Graham family until 1925. The roof of the building was
removed in 1954 but it remains the seat of Clan Graham.

Mugdock Castle, Mugdock Country Park, G62 8EL. Stronghold
of Clan Graham from the mid-13th century. Only ruins
remain.

# GRANT

**Chief of the Name and Arms:**
The Rt Hon. Sir James Grant of that Ilk, 6th Lord Strathspey
**Motto:** 'Stand fast, stand sure'
**Plane Badge:** Pine
www.clangrant.org

Some historians have asserted that the Grants were part of the Siol Alpin group of families who descend from Alpin, father of Kenneth MacAlpin, first king of Scots. The Grant name first appears in Scotland in the 13th century when a Gregory Grant married the daughter and heiress of Sir John Bisset, who brought with her the lands of Stratherrick on the south-eastern shore of Loch Ness. Sir Laurence Grant appears as Sheriff of Inverness in 1263. The clan supported Robert the Bruce and the Grants were confirmed in their holdings in Strathspey.

Staunch Royalists, the Grants of Freuchie allied themselves with the Marquis of Montrose after the Battle of Inverlochy in 1645 and subsequently supported William and Mary and the House of Hanover during the Jacobite Risings of 1715 and 1745.

In 1811, Sir Lewis Grant of Grant inherited the Ogilvie earldoms of Seafield and Findlater (as established in the Celtic tradition of titles passing through the female line). The Grants of Rothiemurchus still hold their lands around Aviemore. In 2011, John Grant of Rothiemurchus succeeded to the earldom of Dysart through his mother.

GRANT HUNTING ANCIENT

## ANCESTRAL INTEREST

Castle Grant, Grantown-on-Spey, PH26 3PS. Originally a
Comyn stronghold and formerly known as Freuchie. Seat of
earls of Seafield.

Duthil, Carrbridge, PH23. Twin Grant mausoleums; Cullen
House, Buckie, AB56 4XW. Former home of earls of
Seafield. Now residential apartments.

Grantown-on-Spey (formerly Castletoun-of-Freuchie). Town
planned by Sir James Grant of Castle Grant in 1776.

Urquhart Castle, Drumnadrochit, Loch Ness, IV63 6XJ. Gifted
by James IV to John Grant of Freuchie in 1509. Grants held
Urquhart for 400 years, despite it being partly blown up to
destroy Jacobite access in 1691.

# HAMILTON

**Chief of the Name and Arms:** His Grace the 16th Duke of
Hamilton and 13th Duke of Brandon
**Motto:** 'Through'
www.clanhamilton.org

The Hamilton family descend from Walter Fitz-Gilbert of Hameldone who was granted the lands of Cadzow, South Lanarkshire, by Robert the Bruce. The surname is thought to have originated from Hamilton in Lanarkshire or possibly from Hambleton in Yorkshire or Lancashire. Walter's son fought for David II at the Battle of Neville's Cross in 1346 and was taken prisoner. James, 1st Lord Hamilton, married Princess Mary Stewart, daughter of James II, and their son was created Earl of Arran.

The 2nd Earl of Arran was Regent of Scotland for Mary, Queen of Scots. His grandson was created Marquis of Hamilton in 1599. James, 3rd Marquis, was created Duke of Hamilton by Charles I in 1643, making him the premier peer of Scotland. He led an army into England in support of Charles but was taken prisoner at the Battle of Preston in 1648.

The titles passed to his daughter Anne, who married William Douglas, Earl of Selkirk, later connecting the dukedom to the Douglas family although the Duke remains Chief of the Hamiltons, NOT the Douglases. Branches of the family include the dukes of Abercorn, and earls of Haddington.

The 14th Duke of Hamilton piloted the first aeroplane over Mount Everest in 1933.

**ANCESTRAL INTEREST**

Brodick Castle, Isle of Arran.
Cadzow Castle, Chatelherault Country Park, Hamilton,
    ML3 7UE.

HAMILTON RED MODERN

Hamilton House, Prestonpans, EH32 9JY. Built for Sir John
    Hamilton in 1626. National Trust for Scotland.
Lennoxlove, Haddington, EH41 4NZ. Current home of the
    dukes of Hamilton. Formerly known as Lethington and
    previously home of the Duke of Lauderdale (Maitland).
Mellerstain, Gordon, Berwickshire, TD3 6LG. William and
    Robert Adam mansion, seat of the earls of Haddington.
Tyninghame, Dunbar, East Lothian, EH42 1XW. Estate acquired
    by Thomas Hamilton in 1628. William Burn built current
    mansion for 9th Earl of Haddington in 1829. Today
    apartments.

71

# HANNAY

**Chief of the Name and Arms:** Dr David R. Hannay
**Motto:** 'Through difficulties to Heaven' (*'Per ardua ad Alta'*)
**Plant Badge:** Periwinkle
The Clan Hannay Society is on Facebook

The Hannay family sprang from the ancient province of Galloway and their earliest known possession was Sorbie Tower which they acquired, possibly through marriage, from the Anglo-Norman family of Vipont, Lords of Westmorland. A Gilbert de Hannethe signed the Ragman Roll in 1296.

The Hannays supported John Balliol who, through his mother the Lady Devorgilla, represented the old Celtic Lords of Galloway. In 1308 they were forced to submit to Edward Bruce when he conquered Galloway for his brother Robert the Bruce. In later years, the Hannays feuded with and sided with the Kennedys, the Dunbars and the Morays, and joined James IV on his pilgrimage to St Ninian's shrine at Whithorn; they supported the Stuart monarchy at the battles of Sauchieburn and Flodden. It was at Dean James Hannay's head that Jenny Geddes in 1637 flung her stool at St Giles' Kirk in protest at the Scottish Book of Common Prayer.

In the 17th century, a deadly feud with the Murrays of Broughton led to the Hannays of Sorbie being outlawed. The outcome was that large numbers of the family emigrated to Antrim, Down and Armagh in Ulster.

72

HANNAY

## ANCESTRAL INTEREST

Kirkdale, Gatehouse of Fleet, Dumfries and Galloway,
DG8 7EA. Ancestral seat of the Hannay family since 1532.
Current house built by Robert Adam.

Sorbie Tower, Newton Stewart, DG8 8AG. Ancient Hannay
fortified stronghold. Ruined since the 18th century.
Restoration is underway by the Clan Hannay Society.

# HAY

**Chief of the Name and Arms:**
The Rt Hon. Merlin Hay, 24th Earl of Erroll
**Motto:** 'Keep the yoke!' (*Serva jugum*)
**Clan Badge**: Mistletoe
www.clanhay.org

William de la Haye from Normandy was a senior leader in William the Conqueror's army when he invaded England in 1066. However, his involvement in this historic enterprise to some extent conflicts with the Hay tradition of the Legend of Luncarty in Scotland c.980, where a countryman of the name Hay and his two sons saved the day for the army of Kenneth III against the invading Danes. As a result, the King commanded that a falcon be set loose from Kinnoull Hill and that the land it flew over be awarded to the heroes of the day.

The lands of Erroll in Perthshire were confirmed on William de la Haye, Cup Bearer to Malcolm IV, in a charter of 1172 and he was cited as an ancestor when Sir William Hay was created Earl of Erroll in 1453. Sir Gilbert Hay fought with Robert the Bruce and was rewarded with the lands of Slains, near Aberdeen, and the honour of becoming hereditary Lord High Constable of Scotland, a post which his descendant retains to this day.

The Hays of Locherworth descend from a younger brother who married into the family of the wizard Hugo de Giffard and acquired the lands of Yester. John Hay was created Baron Yester in 1478, and John, 8th Baron, was created Earl of Tweeddale in 1646. The 2nd Earl, who was Lord Chancellor of Scotland in 1704–05, was created Marquess of Tweeddale. The Hays of Smithfield and Haystoun are Nova Scotia baronetcies awarded by James VI in 1635.

HAY MODERN

## ANCESTRAL INTEREST

Castle of Park, Glenluce, DG8 0AB. Category A listed 16th-century building owned by Landmark Trust.

Duns Castle, Berwickshire, TD11 3NW.

Haystoun House, Peebles, EH45 9JG. Seventeenth-century house. Private home.

Neidpath Castle, Peebles, EH45 8NW. The Barony of Neidpath passed to the Hay family through marriage in 1312 and ownership was held until 1686 when it passed to the Duke of Queensberry. Now belongs to the earls of Wemyss. Neidpath Castle was visited by Mary, Queen of Scots and her son James VI.

# HENDERSON

**Chief of the Name and Arms:** Alistair Henderson of Fordell
**Motto:** 'Virtue alone ennobles' (*Sola virtus nobilitat*)
**Plant Badge:** Cotton grass
www.clanhendersonsociety.com

 The Highland Clan of Henderson (Mackendrick) held lands encompassing Glencoe, Argyll and claimed descent from Eanruig Mor Mac Righ Neachtain, a Pictish prince. They became hereditary pipers to Clan Abrach. The direct line is believed to have ended with an heiress, but through marriage the Hendersons became part of the Macdonald Clan Iain of Glencoe. Their last chief was therefore killed at the Massacre of Glencoe in 1692.

The senior Lowland family of the name resided at Fordell Castle, near Inverkeithing in Fife. They claim descent from the ancient Dumfriesshire family of Henryson. William Henrison was chamberlain of Lochmaben Castle in the 14th century. Alexander Henderson of Fordell was violently opposed to Charles I's attempts to reform the Church of Scotland and, along with Archibald Johnston of Warriston, drafted the National Covenant in 1638, and five years later, the Solemn League and Covenant.

## ANCESTRAL INTEREST

Fordell Castle, Dunfermline, Fife, KY4 8EX. Seventeenth-century tower. Privately owned.

Glencoe Visitor Centre, Ballachulish, PH49 4HX. The notorious Massacre of Glencoe took place on 13 February 1692. The MacIain MacDonalds of Glencoe were murdered by a Government regiment which had been quartered on them

76

under instructions from Lord Stair. MacDonald of Glencoe had delayed in swearing allegiance to William and Mary in place of James VIII. The Glencoe Visitor Centre is maintained by the National Trust for Scotland.

Lochmaben Castle, Lockerbie, DG11 1JE. An important outpost in the defence of Scotland against England. Historic Environment Scotland.

# HOME

**Chief of the Name and Arms:** David Alexander Cospatrick
Douglas-Home, the Earl of Home KT, CVO
**Motto:** 'True to the end'
**Plant Badge:** Broom

 Aidan de Home acquired his name from the lands
of Home in Berwickshire and was descended in
the male line from Cospatric, Earl of Dunbar, the
Anglo-Celtic lord who lived in the 11th century.
His descendant, Sir Thomas, married the heiress
of Dunglass and their eldest son succeeded as
chief while their younger son founded the Homes
of Wedderburn. The Barony of Home was created in 1473. The
Homes supported James IV at the Battle of Flodden in 1513. After
the battle, he resisted the regency of John Stewart, Duke of
Albany, and was captured and executed for rebellion.

When James VI travelled into England in 1603, he stopped
off at Dunglass Castle and Alexander, 6th Lord Home,
accompanied him south to his coronation. Alexander was created
Earl of Home in 1605. During the Jacobite Rising of 1715, the 7th
Earl was imprisoned in Edinburgh Castle and his Dunglass estate
was forfeited. During the Jacobite Rising of 1745, the 8th Earl
supported the British Government, fighting with Sir John Cope's
soldiers at the Battle of Prestonpans. He was subsequently
appointed Governor of Gibralter.

In the 20th century, the 14th Earl of Home served as Prime
Minister of the United Kingdom from 1963 to 1964.

## ANCESTRAL INTEREST

Dunglass, Cockburnspath, TD13 5XF. Charter of Collegiate
Church granted to Alexander Home in 1423.

Fast Castle, Coldingham, TD14 5TY. Built as Home coastal
stronghold, possibly as early as the 13th century. Ruins
accessible, but care should be taken on the cliffs.

The Hirsel, Coldstream, Berwickshire, TD12 4LP. Seat of the
earls of Home. Gardens seasonally open to the public.

Hume Castle, Berwickshire, TD5 7TR. Once seat of the earls of
Home. Hume Castle Preservation Trust.

# HUNTER

**Chief of the Name and Arms:**
Madam Pauline Hunter of Hunterston
**Motto:** 'I have completed the course' (*Cursum perficio*')
**Plant Badge:** Sea pink (*Armeria maritima*)
www.clanhunterusa.org, www.clanhunterscotland.com

 This family arrived in the west coast of Scotland from Normandy and England c.1110. Aylmer de Hunter signed the Ragman Roll of 1296, and the lands of Hunter were granted to William Hunter by Robert II in 1374. By the 15th century, the Hunters of Hunterston had been appointed hereditary keepers of the royal forests of Arran and Little Cumbrae.

John, 14th Laird, died with James IV at the Battle of Flodden in 1513. Mungo, 16th Laird, was killed at the Battle of Pinkie in 1547. Robert, a grandson of the 20th Laird, became Governor of Virginia, and subsequently of New York.

In 1954, the Hunterston estate passed through marriage to the Cochran-Patrick family and, in 1969, Neil Cochran-Patrick was recognised by the Lord Lyon as 29th Chief in the undifferenced arms of Hunter of Hunterston (exclusive to bearer).

## ANCESTRAL INTEREST

Hunterian Museum, Glasgow, G12 8QQ. Contents donated by the physician William Hunter (1718–83).

Hunter's Quay, Dunoon, PA23 8JW. Named after the Hunters of Hafton House who in the 19th century bought up this coastline. Now Hunters Quay Holiday Village.

Hunterston Castle, West Kilbride, KA23 9QG. A fortified keep dating from the late 15th century. The ancestral home of the Hunter family.

HUNTER/MITCHELL/GALBRAITH/RUSSELL MODERN

Hunterston estate, West Kilbride, KA23 9QG. The atomic
 energy station is situated on the lands of Hunterston.
Hunterston House, West Kilbride, KA23 9QG. Neoclassical
 mansion adjacent to Hunterston Castle. It was built for the
 Hunter family in the 19th century.

# IRVINE

**Chief of the Name and Arms:**
Alexander Irvine of Drum, 27th Baron of Drum
**Motto:** 'Flourishing both in sunshine and shade'
('*Sub sole sub umbra virens*')
www.irvineclan.com

A territorial surname taken from Irving, an old parish in Dumfriesshire. Tradition suggests that the senior branch of the family originated from the High Kings of Ireland through the Abbots of Dunkeld. The Irvines followed Robert the Bruce, William de Irwin becoming armour bearer to the King for which he was rewarded the royal forest of Drum.

Clan Irvine was much preoccupied in feuds against Clan Keith during the 15th century, culminating in the Battle of Drumoak in 1402. At the Battle of Harlaw in 1411, Alexander Irvine faced Hector of the Battles Maclean and both died of their wounds. During the Anglo-Scottish wars, the 6th Laird's son was killed at the Battle of Pinkie in 1547. During the Jacobite Risings of the 18th century, Clan Irvine supported the Jacobites at the Battle of Sheriffmuir in 1715 and Battle of Culloden in 1746.

In 2002, the Chief of Clan Irvine entered into a peace treaty with the 13th Earl of Kintore, Chief of Clan Keith, thus ending a 600-year feud.

IRVINE MUTED

### ANCESTRAL INTEREST

Bonshaw Tower, Lockerbie, DG11 3LY. Oblong tower house built
    in the 16th century and situated near Gretna Green. Seat of
    the Irvine family for 900 years.

Drum Castle, Banchory, AB31 5EY. The Royal Forest and Tower
    of Drum were given to the Irvine family in 1323. Later a
    Jacobean mansion house was added with Victorian
    extensions. National Trust for Scotland.

# JARDINE

**Chief of the Name and Arms:**
Sir William Murray Jardine, 13th Baronet of Applegarth
**Motto:** 'Beware, I am coming!' ('*Cave adsum*')
**Plant Badge:** Apple blossom

The Du Jardine name is recorded at the Battle of Hastings in 1066 and it is assumed that in the aftermath the family initially settled in the vicinity of Kendal in the 12th century before moving to the Wandel and Hartside area of Lanarkshire. By the 14th century they were established at Applegirth in Dumfriesshire where they have remained ever since.

The Jardines followed the powerful Borders family of Johnston and supported Mary, Queen of Scots until her marriage to Lord Bothwell, transferring their allegiance to her son James VI. Sir Alexander Irvine married Lady Margaret Douglas, sister of the Duke of Queensberry, and in 1672 their son was created a Nova Scotia baronet by Charles II.

The Buchanan-Jardines of Castle Milk in Dumfriesshire descend from Robert Jardine, head of Jardine, Matheson & Co, the Hong Kong-based merchant trading company founded in 1832.

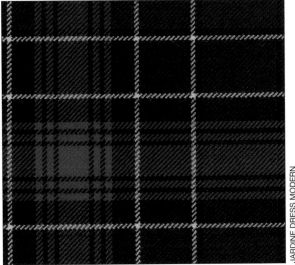

**ANCESTRAL INTEREST**

Spedlins Tower, Lochmaben, DG11 1EW. Abandoned in the late
17th century, allegedly to escape a ghost, this fine large tower
house has been restored. Nearby, on the left bank of the
River Annan, was Jardine Hall, designed by James Gillespie
Graham, but this was demolished in 1964.

# JOHNSTON (E)

**Chief of the Name and Arms:** Patrick Andrew Wentworth
Hope-Johnstone, the 11th Earl of Annandale and Hartfell
**Motto:** 'Never unprepared' (*'Nunquam non paratus'*)
**Plant Badge:** Red hawthorn
www.clanjohnstone.org

Once an extremely powerful Border Reiver clan,
the Johnston(e)s held sway over the central area of
Annandale and, in 1643, Sir James of that Ilk was
created Earl of Hartfell. The legend is that the
Chief of the Johnstons, while at the Scottish
Court, heard of the English King's planned
treachery to dispose of Robert the Bruce in favour
of his rival Balliol. He promptly sent Bruce a spur and a feather
tied to it to indicate 'flight at speed'. Bruce acted on the warning.

The Johnstones were intermittently appointed Wardens of
the Western Marches, defending the Borders from English
raiders and alternating with the Maxwells with whom they
entered into a deadly feud.

James Johnstone was created Lord Johnstone of Lochwood
by Charles I in 1633, and Earl of Hartfell in 1643. He fought for
the Marquis of Montrose but was captured at the Battle of
Philiphaugh. His son was created Earl of Annandale by Charles
II. The 3rd Earl of Hartfell, 2nd Earl of Annandale and Hartfell,
President of the Privy Council, was created Marquess of
Annandale in 1701. The family titles became dormant with the
3rd Marquess's death in 1792.

Almost 200 years later, in 1982, the Lord Lyon recognised
Major Percy Johnstone of Annandale of that Ilk as Baron of the
lands and earldom of Annandale. In 1985, he was recognised as
Chief of the Name and Arms of Johnstone.

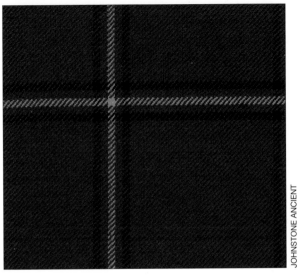

**ANCESTRAL INTEREST**

Lochwood Tower, Moffat, DG10 9PS. Burned by the Maxwells
  and Armstrongs in 1593. Abandoned in 1724.
Raehills, Lockerbie, DG11 1HL. William Burn mansion. Home
  of the earls of Annandale and Hartfell.

# KEITH

**Chief of the Name and Arms:**
Sir James Falconer Keith of Urie, 14th Earl of Kintore
**Motto:** 'Truth prevails' (*'Veritas vincit'*)
**Plant Badge:** White rose
www.clankeith-usa.org

Both a Highland and Lowland clan, the Keiths historically held the hereditary title of Marischal, then Great Marischal, then Earl Marischal of Scotland. Tradition has it that an ancestor fought for Malcolm II at the Battle of Barry in 1010.

For their support of Robert the Bruce, Robert de Keith was granted the royal forest of Halforest and lands of Kintore. His nephew William Keith of Galston accompanied the heart of Robert the Bruce to Spain on a Crusade and, following the deaths of Sir James Douglas and his cohorts at the Battle of Teba in Andalucia, returned the casket to Melrose Abbey in 1331.

Sir William Keith the Marischal married the heiress of Sir Alexander Fraser, acquiring estates in Buchan, Kincardine and Lothian. His brother John married the Cheyne heiress who brought the family Inverugie Castle. Three of Sir William's children married children of Robert II. The third son of the 6th Earl Marischal was created Earl of Kintore for his role in saving the Scottish regalia from Oliver Cromwell. The 10th Earl Marischal supported the Old Pretender in 1715 and, as a result, was stripped of the title and it passed to the Falconer family. In 1801, the Lord Lyon recognised Keith of Ravelston and Dunotter as representative of the Marischal Keiths. In 1978, the Chief of Clan Keith signed a treaty with the Commander of Clan Gunn, ending a clan feud which had begun in 1478.

KEITH MODERN

## ANCESTRAL INTEREST

Dunnottar Castle, Stonehaven, AB39 2TL. Dramatic clifftop ruins surrounded on three sides by the North Sea. Scottish regalia was taken here for safekeeping in the 17th century.

Keith Marischal, Humbie, East Lothian, EH36 5PA. Sixteenth-century baronial house first built by 5th Earl Marischal in 1589. Sold in 1889. Private residence.

Peterhead, Aberdeenshire. The town was founded in 1593 by George Keith, 5th Earl Marischal. The statue in front of the Town House is of James Keith, brother of the 10th Earl Marischal who became a Marshall in the army of Frederick the Great of Prussia.

# KENNEDY

**Chief of the Name and Arms:**
The Most Hon. David Kennedy, 9th Marquess of Ailsa
**Motto:** 'Consider the end' (*'Avise la fin'*)
**Plant Badge:** Oak
www.kennedysociety.net

A Galloway/Ayrshire family, descendants of Duncan of Carrick who lived in the 12th century. They supported Robert the Bruce in the Wars of Scottish Independence. James of Dunure married Mary, daughter of Robert III, and their son Sir Gilbert was one of the six regents of Scotland during the minority of James III. He was created Lord Kennedy in 1457.

David, 3rd Lord Kennedy, was created Earl of Cassilis in 1509 and was killed at the Battle of Flodden in 1513. Gilbert, 2nd Earl, was assassinated in 1527 by Sir Hugh Campbell of Loudoun, Sheriff of Ayr, over a land dispute.

In 1570, a dispute over the ownership of abbey lands arose between Gilbert Kennedy, 4th Earl of Cassilis, and Allan Stewart, Commendator of Crossraguel Abbey. When Stewart refused to sign over the lands, Cassilis had him roasted over a brazier until he agreed. He never walked again.

The 6th and 7th Earls of Cassilis were staunch supporters of the Scottish parliament during the Wars of the Three Kingdoms. Archibald, 12th Earl of Cassilis, was created Marquess of Ailsa in 1831.

## ANCESTRAL INTEREST

Castle Kennedy, Stranraer, DG9 8SL. Built by the Earl of Cassilis
in 1607. Passed to the Earl of Stair in 1716 and replaced by
Lochinch Castle.

Culzean Castle, Maybole, KA19 8LE. Today it is the clifftop
'jewel in the crown' of the National Trust for Scotland. Built
by architect Robert Adam for the 10th Earl of Cassilis on the
site of an ancient Kennedy castle.

Dunure Castle, Dunure, KA7 4LW. Original 13th-century
stronghold of the Kennedys of Carrick.

# KERR

**Chief of the Name and Arms:**
The Most Hon. Michael Kerr, 13th Marquess of Lothian
**Motto:** 'Late but in earnest' (*Sero sed serio*)
**Plane Badge:** Bog myrtle
www.clankerr.co.uk

Thought to be of Norse descent, the family first appeared in the valley of the Jed Water in the Scottish Borders in the 14th century. Sir Andrew Kerr of Ferniehirst was appointed Warden of the Middle Marches in 1502. Andrew Kerr of Cessford was similarly appointed in 1513. Sir Andrew Kerr of Cessford was killed near Melrose while escorting the infant James V to Edinburgh in 1526.

At the time of the Reformation, Mark Kerr, Commendator of Newbattle Abbey, had his lands erected into a barony by a charter in 1591. He was created Earl of Lothian in 1606. Sir Andrew Kerr of Ferniehirst was created Lord Jedburgh in 1621. Robert Kerr followed James VI to London and was created Earl of Ancram. The history of rivalry between the two Kerr houses of Cessford and Ferniehirst is complex, with one branch becoming earls and marquesses of Lothian; the other, earls and dukes of Roxburghe, with the titles of the latter passing through the female line to the Innes family.

Two sons of the 3rd Marquess of Lothian fought against the Jacobites at the Battle of Culloden, one being killed and his elder brother commanding three squadrons of Hanoverian Cavalry. The survivor went on to serve under the Duke of Cumberland in France in 1758.

KERR RED MODERN

## ANCESTRAL INTEREST

Ferniehirst Castle, Jedburgh, TD8 6NX. A lovingly restored 15th-century castle owned by the Lothian family. It is available to rent.

Monteviot House, Jedburgh, TD8 6UQ. Family home of the Marquess of Lothian. Gardens open to the public.

Newbattle Abbey, Dalkeith, EH22 3LL. Abbey built in 1140 for Cistercian monks under David I. Modified and rebuilt by architects John Mylne in 1650, William Burn in 1836 and David Bryce in 1858. It was visited by George IV in 1822, but given to the nation by the 11th Marquess of Lothian in 1937 for use as a college of education.

# KINCAID

**Chief of the Name and Arms:**
Madam Arabella Kincaid of Kincaid
**Motto**: 'This I'll defend'
www.clankincaid.org

Of territorial origin, the surname is closely connected with the Comyn Lords of Badenoch and earldom of Lennox. In 1296 the Laird of Kincaid was party to the recapture of Edinburgh Castle from Edward I and was made constable of Edinburgh Castle, an office he held until 1314.

Through marriage, the Kincaids acquired the estate of Craiglockhart in Edinburgh, and lands near Falkirk and Linlithgow. They fought on the Royalist side during the Wars of the Three Kingdoms, campaigning largely in Ireland. As a result, a large number of the surname emigrated to North America.

The Kincaids supported the Stuart cause and, following the 1715 Jacobite Rising, David Kincaid of Kincaid was obliged to go into exile. He settled in Virginia, as did four sons of Alexander Kincaid after the Battle of Culloden.

In 1959, Alwyne Cecil Peareth Kincaid-Lennox petitioned the Lord Lyon King of Arms to succeed to the coat of arms of his great-great-grandfather John Kincaid of Kincaid, and was recognised as Chief of the Name of Kincaid. In 2001, Arabella Kincaid Lennox matriculated her coat of arms and assumed the name Kincaid of Kincaid.

KINCAID ANCIENT

## ANCESTRAL INTEREST

Blackness Castle, Linlithgow, EH49 7NH. Built by Sir George
Crichton in the mid-15th century, this was acquired by the
Kincaids through marriage but fell to Oliver Cromwell
during his invasion of 1650. Historic Environment Scotland.

Craigmaddie Castle, Mugdock, G62 8LB. Held by the Kincaids
in the Middle Ages. Only ruins remain. Historic
Environment Scotland.

# LAMONT

**Chief of the Name and Arms:**
The Rev. Fr. Peter Noel Lamont of that Ilk
**Motto:** 'Neither spare nor dispose' (*Ne parcas nec spernas*)
**Plant Badge:** Crab-apple tree
www.clanlamontsociety.com

The Lamont surname is Old Norse for 'Lawmen'. The Clan Lamont is traditionally descended from the Irish royal house of O'Neill and founded by a descendant of Fearchar, Mormaer of Ross, in the 13th century. At one time, the family owned the greater portion of the Cowal peninsula in Argyll.

Like their MacDougall neighbours to the north, the Lamonts opposed Robert the Bruce and suffered accordingly. However, John Lamont of that Ilk subsequently held a charter from James III for his clan seat Toward Castle. All was well until the 17th century when Sir James Lamont of Inveryne supported the Marquis of Montrose in the Royalist cause, carrying 'fire and sword' into Campbell country. Both the Lamont strongholds of Toward Castle on Cowal and Ascog Castle at Tighnabruaich were destroyed by the Marquis of Argyll. Both castles surrendered following promises of life and liberty, but the Campbells slaughtered 'the whole gentlemen of the name Lamont'. On the Restoration of Charles II, Argyll was executed in Edinburgh.

The remainder of the Lamont lands on Cowal was sold by the family in 1893, and the 21st Chief emigrated to Australia where his descendant, the 29th Chief, remains. The Clan Lamont Society was formed in 1895 in Glasgow.

LAMONT ANCIENT

## ANCESTRAL INTEREST

Ardlamont House, Tighnabruaich, Argyll, PA21 2AH. Mansion built for Major General John Lamont, 19th Chief, in 1820.

Ascog Castle, Tighnabruaich, Argyll, PA21 2DA. Ruined 15th-century stronghold of Clan Lamont.

Clan Lamont Memorial, Dunoon, Argyll, PA23 7HP. A memorial erected in 1906 by the Clan Lamont Society to commemorate the many Lamonts killed in the massacre of 1646.

Toward Castle, Dunoon, PA23 7UG. Fifteenth-century ruin destroyed by the Marquis of Argyll in 1646.

# LESLIE

**Chief of the Name and Arms:** The Hon. Alexander Leslie
**Motto:** 'Grip fast'
**Plant Badge:** Rue
www.clanlesliesociety.org

The clan is descended from Bartolf, a Hungarian nobleman who arrived in Scotland in 1067 as a follower of Edgar Atheling, brother of Queen (St) Margaret, wife of Malcolm III. The king bestowed upon him estates in Fife, Angus and Aberdeenshire and appointed him governor of Edinburgh Castle. Through marriage, the Leslies acquired the baronies of Rothes, Fytekill and Ballinbreich. George Leslie of Rothes and Fytekill was created Earl of Rothes in 1457, and John, 6th Earl, was created Duke of Rothes in 1680. On his death, the dukedom became extinct but the earldom continued in the female line.

Sir Alexander Leslie, having served with the Swedish army, in which he attained the rank of Field Marshal in 1638, took command of the Covenanters army and defeated the King's troops in various engagements. At the treaty of peace, signed in 1641, he was created Lord Balgonie and Earl of Leven. Sir Alexander Leslie of Auchintoul became a General in the Russian Army and was appointed Governor of Smolensk.

The 9th Earl was Vice Admiral of Scotland and Governor of Stirling Castle. He was a staunch Hanoverian and commanded a regiment of cavalry at the Battle of Sheriffmuir in 1715. The majority of the Rothes estates were sold.

LESLIE RED MODERN

**ANCESTRAL INTEREST**

Balgonie Castle, Markinch, Glenrothes, KY7 6HQ. Fifteenth-century tower reconstructed by Alexander Earl of Leven. Sold in 1824. Today home of Laird of Balgonie and Edergoll.

Balquhain Castle, Inverurie, AB51 5HB. Sixteenth-century ruined tower. Historic Environment Scotland.

Leslie Castle, Insch, AB52 6NX. Historic seat of Clan Leslie. Refurbished by architect David Carnegie Leslie in 1980. Today a guest house.

Pitcairlie House, Auchtermuchty, KY14 6EU. Owned by Clan Leslie from 16th century.

Pitcaple Castle, Inverurie, AB51 5HL. Built for the Leslies but passed through marriage to the Lumsdens.

# LINDSAY

**Chief of the Name and Arms:** Robert Lindsay, 29th Earl of Crawford and 12th Earl of Balcarres
**Motto:** 'Endure bravely' (*Endure fort*)
www.clanlindsaysociety.co.uk

Sir Walter de Lindsay, of Norman descent, is among those who accompanied David, Earl of Huntingdon, to Scotland to claim his throne. In 1180, Sir Walter was created Baron of Luffness and Laird of Crawford, having acquired significant wealth through his marriage to Ethelreda, granddaughter of Gospatric of Northumbria.

Sir David Lindsay of Crawford acquired Glenesk in Angus c.1340 through marriage to Maria Abernethy. They had two sons: David, who was created Earl of Crawford in 1398 and married a daughter of Robert II, and Sir William of the Byres. John, 10th Lord Lindsay of the Byres, a descendant of the 6th Baron Crawford, was created Earl of Lindsay in 1366.

The Lindsays of Edzell descend from a son of the 9th Earl of Crawford. The Lindsays of Balcarres descend from a younger son of the 9th Earl of Crawford. The first Earl of Balcarres was made hereditary governor of Edinburgh Castle and Secretary of State for Scotland.

In 1540, Sir David Lindsay of the Mount gained fame through being author of *Ane Satyre of the Thrie Estaitis*, which poked fun at Church and State.

**ANCESTRAL INTEREST**

Balcarres House, Colinsburgh, KY9 1HN. Ancestral seat of the
earls of Crawford and Balcarres. Built by John Lindsay in
1595.

Ceres Parish Church, Cupar, KY15 5NA. The medieval
mausoleum of the Crawfords adjoins the church.

Edzell Castle, Brechin, DD9 7UE. Ruined ancestral home of
Clan Lindsay. Sold in 1715. Historic Environment Scotland.

# LIVINGSTON (MACLEA)

**Chief of the Name and Arms**
The Much Hon. Niall Livingstone of Bachuil,
Baron of the Bachuil
**Motto:** 'I shall do it if I can' (*Ni mi e ma's urrain dhomh*)
Maclea: 'If I can' (*Si je puis*)
**Plant Badge**: Grass of parnassus
www.clanlivingstone.info

 Leving, a Saxon, held lands in West Lothian in the 12th century and these became known as Leving's-toun. Members of this family were prominent in Scotland's history between 1300 and 1715, and held several peerages, notably the earldoms of Callendar, Linlithgow and Newburgh. The Linlithgow earldom was attainted after the 1715 Jacobite Rising.

The small Highland clan of Livingstone from the Isle of Lismore and western Argyll originally carried a Gaelic name spelled in different ways – Mac Dhunnshleibhe, Mac-an-Leigh, or MacLea – closely associated with the Stewarts of Appin.

In the mid-17th century, James Livingston of Skirling was granted a ten-year lease of the bishoprics of Argyll and the Isles. He took up residence on Lismore and it is thought that, as a result, the surname of Livingstone was adopted by Clan MacLea. St Moluag was a missionary and contemporary of St Columba in the 6th century.

In 1950, Livingstone of Bachuil was recognised by the Lord Lyon King of Arms as the Coarb, or hereditary keeper, of the pastoral staff of St Moluag. It is is said to have miraculous healing powers.

**ANCESTRAL INTEREST**

Bachuil, Lismore, PA34 5UL. Ancestral home of the Livingstones of Bachuil.

Callendar House, Falkirk, FK1 1YR. The oldest part of the house was built by the Livingstone family in the 14th century. Visited by Mary, Queen of Scots, Prince Charles Edward Stuart and Queen Victoria. Bought by William Forbes in 1783. Today owned by Falkirk Community Trust.

David Livingstone Centre, Blantyre, G72 9BY. Birthplace museum celebrating the life and times of the legendary explorer and missionary David Livingstone.

# MACALISTER

**Chief of the Name and Arms**: William Somerville McAlester of
Loup and Kennox, Mac Iain Duibh
**Motto**: *'Fortiter'*
**Plant Badge**: Heath
www.clanmacalistersociety.org

 A branch of Clan Donald which traces its
ancestry to a great-grandson of Somerled. Clan
lands were in Kintyre and the clan seat was on the
north-west side of West Loch Tarbert. A later seat
was Loup, and these lands were held by the clan
until the early 19th century. The MacAlisters were
numerically strong on Bute and Arran, and the
chiefs were constables of Tarbert Castle on Loch Fyne.

There were turbulent times for the MacAlisters during the
16th and 17th centuries. In 1600, MacAlister clansfolk invaded
the Isle of Arran and soon after raided the Isle of Bute. Alexander
MacAlister and Angus Og MacDonald of Islay were found guilty
of treason and executed. Some clan members moved to Stirling
and anglicised their name to Alexander. William Alexander
acquired the estate of Menstrie and, through connections with
Stirling Castle and James VI, was closely involved in the
colonisation of Scottish territories in Canada.

Most of the MacAlister lands in Knapdale and Kintyre were
confiscated by the Earl of Argyll after the 1745 Jacobite Rising. In
1792 Charles, 12th of Loup, married the daughter and heiress of
William Somerville of Kennox and the family seat removed to
Ayrshire. In 1796, Colonel Matthew MacAlister purchased
Glenbarr Abbey.

MACALISTER ANCIENT

## ANCESTRAL INTEREST

Glenbarr Abbey, Kintyre, PA29 6UT. Purchased in 1796 by 1st Laird of Glenbarr and extended in early 18th century. Gifted to Clan MacAlister in 1986. Now the Clan MacAlister Visitor Centre.

Kennox House, Stewarton. Built by Earl of Somerville *c.*1690. Ancestral seat of Clan MacAlister.

Tarbert Castle, PA29 6UD. Strategic medieval royal castle, now a ruin.

Torrisdale Castle, Campbeltown, PA28 6QT. Built in 1815 for General Keith Macalister, son of Ranald Macalister of Glenbarr.

# MACBEAN (MACBAIN)

**Chief of the Name and Arms:** James McBain of McBain
**Motto:** 'Touch not a catt' (*Bot a targe*)
**Plant Badge:** Boxwood
www.clanmacbean.org

The MacBeans are thought to have originated in Lochaber and settled in eastern Inverness-shire. Myles MacBean supported Mackintosh against the Red Comyn and the principal family of the surname was MacBean of Kinchyle. The MacBean territory lay chiefly in the Parish of Dores and the clan represented by MacBeans of Kinchyle, Faillie and Tomatin was closely associated with the Clan Chattan tribal federation.

Clan MacBean fought for the Lord of the Isles at the Battle of Harlaw in 1411 and suffered heavy losses. The 12th Chief incurred serious debts and was obliged to sell his lands in 1685. Many clansfolk of MacBean supported the Jacobite Rising of 1715 and as a result were captured and transported to Virginia, Maryland and South Carolina. Gillies MacBean, standing 6ft 4in tall, was killed at the Battle of Culloden in 1746.

In 1959, Hughston MacBain, an American descended from a younger son of Aeneas and Gillies MacBean, of the Kinchyle branch, was acknowledged as Chief of the Name by the Lord Lyon King of Arms.

**ANCESTRAL INTEREST**

MacBean Memorial Park, Kinchyle, IV2 6DP. Created by
  Hughston M. MacBain, 21st Chief of Clan MacBean in 1961.
  'Dedicated to the Memory of the Clan MacBean (MacBain)
  of long ago whose ancient chiefs once owned extensive lands
  in this area.'

# MACDONALD (CLAN DONALD)

www.clandonald.org; www.clandonaldusa.org

 The largest and oldest of the Highland and Island clans originates from Conn of the Hundred Battles, Ard Righ of Ireland, in the 1st century AD. In the 12th century, Conn's descendant Somerled, Lord of Argyll, married the daughter of Olaf the Red of Norway. Their descendants include the MacDougalls of Argyll and Lorn, and Clan Donald, sometimes known as the MacDonalds of Islay. There are five Chiefs of Clan Donald under the High Chief, Macdonald of Macdonald.

## ANCESTRAL INTEREST

Dunyvaig Castle, PA43. Ruined seat of MacDonalds of Islay and Kintyre.

Finlaggan, Isle of Islay. PA45 7QL. Ruins of the ancestral residence of the Lords of the Isles.

Glencoe: Memorial to the MacIan MacDonalds of Glencoe who perished in the Massacre of 1692. Sculpted by Macdonald of Aberdeen 1883.

Glencoe Visitor Centre, Ballachulish, PH49 4HX.

MACDONALD MODERN

# MACDONALD OF MACDONALD

**High Chief:** Baron Macdonald of Macdonald
**Motto:** 'By sea and by land' (*Per mare per terras*)

In 1766, Sir Alexander Macdonald was created Lord Macdonald of Macdonald. In 1947, Alexander Macdonald was granted undifferenced arms of Macdonald of Macdonald by the Lord Lyon King of Arms, recognising him as High Chief and 34th Hereditary Chief of Clan Donald.

## ANCESTRAL INTEREST

Aros Castle, Isle of Mull, PA72 6JH.

The Clan Donald Centre, Armadale Castle, Isle of Skye, IV45 8RS, www.armadalecastle.com.

Duntulm Castle, Trotternish, IV51 9UF and Knock Castle, Sleat, Isle of Skye. Both ruins.

Grave of Flora MacDonald, Kilmuir Cemetery, Portree, Isle of Skye, IV51 9YU.

Kildonan Castle, Isle of Arran, KA27 8SD.

MACDONALD LORD OF THE ISLES MODERN

# MACDONALD OF SLEAT

**Chief**: Sir Ian Bosville Macdonald of Sleat
**Motto**: 'By sea and by land' (*Per mare per terras*)

 Founded by Hugh, a 6th great-grandson of
Somerled. Sir Donald, 8th of Sleat and 1st
Baronet of Sleat, was created a Baronet of Nova
Scotia in 1625. The 4th Baronet supported the
Jacobite Rising of 1745 and the Sleat clan lands
were confiscated.

**ANCESTRAL INTEREST**

Dunscaith Castle, Isle of Skye, IV44 8QL. Ruined 'Fortress of
Shadows'.

MACDONALD OF SLEAT MODERN

# MACDONALD OF CLANRANALD

**Chief:** Ranald Macdonald of Clanranald, Captain of Clanranald
**Motto:** 'My hope is constant in thee'

Descended from Reginald, 4th great-grandson of Somerled. Supported the Marquis of Montrose at Battle of Inverlochy in 1645. Clansmen fought for the Jacobite cause at Battle of Prestonpans in 1745 and Battle of Culloden in 1746.

### ANCESTRAL INTEREST

Castle Tioram, Loch Moidart, Lochaber. Ruined ancestral seat of Clanranald.

MACDONALD OF CLANRANALD ANCIENT

# MACDONALD OF KEPPOCH

**Chief:** Ranald Alasdair Macdonald of Keppoch
**Motto:** 'By sea and land' (*'Ai muirs air tir'*)

Descended from a younger son of Good John of Islay, Lord of the Isles, 6th Chief of Clan Donald. Keppoch supported the Jacobite cause in 1715 and 1745, with the 17th Chief dying at the Battle of Culloden in 1746.

## ANCESTRAL INTEREST

Keppoch Castle, Spean Bridge, PH31. Demolished in 1663.

MACDONALD OF KEPPOCH MODERN

# MACDONNELL OF GLENGARRY

**Chief**: Colin Patrick MacDonnell of Glengarry
**Motto**: 'The raven's rock' (*'Creag an fhitich'*)

Descended from Donald of Islay, Somerled's grandson. MacDonnell clansfolk suffered badly from the Highland Clearances of the 18th century but many found a new life in Canada. The family lands were sold in 1828.

## ANCESTRAL INTEREST

Invergarry Castle, PH35 4HW. Ruined stronghold of the
    MacDonnells of Glengarry.
Sir Henry Raeburn's splendid portrait of Colonel Alexander
    (Alastair) MacDonell of Glengarry (1771–1828) can be seen in
    the Scottish National Portrait Gallery, Edinburgh, EH2 1JD
    (www.nationalgalleries.org).
Strome Castle, Loch Carron, Strathcarron, IV54 8YJ. Now a ruin.

MACDONALD OF GLENGARRY MODERN

# MACDOUGALL

**Chief of the Name and Arms:**
Morag MacDougall of MacDougall and Dunollie
**Motto:** 'Victory or death' (*Buaidh no bàs*)
**Plant Badge:** Bell heather
www.macdougall.org

Dougall, sometimes known as Dugald, son of Somerled, originated this clan in the 12th century and styled himself 'King of the South Isles'. In the 13th century, the MacDougall Lords of Argyll and Lorne (sharing common ancestry with the chiefs of Clan Donald) were the most powerful clan in the western Highlands.

However, MacDougall of Lorne was on the losing side in the contest for the Scottish Crown between Robert the Bruce and the Comyns. Sir Alexander MacDougall was married to a sister of John Comyn, Lord of Badenoch, and in consequence, the MacDougall clan after Bruce's victory was deprived of its lands which included Lorne and Benderloch. They were never to regain their island possessions such as Jura, Mull, Lismore, Coll and Tiree, but were re-granted some of their mainland territories when John MacDougall of Lorne married Robert the Bruce's granddaughter.

The MacDougalls supported the Jacobite cause and in 1715 the MacDougall Chief's wife defended Dunollie Castle against government troops while her husband was away fighting at the Battle of Sheriffmuir. The estate was confiscated but returned to the clan in the next generation.

## ANCESTRAL INTEREST

Ardchattan Priory, Oban, PA37 1RQ. Site of Valliscaulian
    monastic community founded by Duncan MacDougall,

Lord of Argyll, in 1230. West end of property converted into private residence.

Dunollie House, Oban, PA34 5TT. Owned by MacDougall of Dunollie Preservation Trust. Ruins of 12th century. The Dunollie Castle and MacDougall Museum are in the grounds.

Dunstaffnage Castle and Chapel, Oban, PA37 1PZ. Partly ruined castle held by the MacDougalls of Lorne in the 13th century but acquired by Clan Campbell. Historic Environment Scotland.

Gylen Castle, Kerrera, Oban, PA34 4SX. Built by Duncan MacDougall in the 16th century. Ruined tower house on island decimated by Covenanters.

# MACGREGOR

**Chief of the Name and Arms:** Sir Malcolm MacGregor of MacGregor, 7th baronet of Lanrick and Balquhidder
**Motto:** 'Royal is my race'
**Plant Badge:** Scots pine
www.clangregor.com

 The senior branch of Clan Alpin, descended from Griogar, third son of Kenneth MacAlpine, King of Scots, in the 9th century. At one time the clan held extensive territories in Perthshire and Argyllshire – in Glenstrae, Glenlochy, Glenlyon and Glengyle. Over time the MacGregors were systematically relieved of their lands by the all-powerful Clan Campbell and, in defiance, became raiders and outlaws.

In 1603, Clan Gregor won a bloody victory over the Colquhouns at Glen Fruin. The Colquhouns held the Royal commission and it was considered an act of rebellion for which the perpetrators were outlawed and hunted down. Over this period, many clansmen changed their surname to avoid capture and became collectively known as the 'Children of the Mist'.

When the Marquis of Montrose raised Charles I's Standard in 1644, the Laird of MacGregor rallied to the cause. However, the clan was not restored to its rightful name until 1775. The best known clansman was Rob Roy MacGregor (1671–1734), immortalised in 1817 by Sir Walter Scott in the novel *Rob Roy*.

MACGREGOR HUNTING MODERN

## ANCESTRAL INTEREST

Glen Fruin, eastern side of Loch Lomond, Argyll & Bute, G84 9EB. Hundreds of Colquhouns and onlookers were massacred here by Clan Gregor in 1603.

Glengyle House, Trossachs, FK8 3UA. Alleged birthplace of Rob Roy MacGregor.

Inchcailloch, Balmaha, G63 0JQ. Loch Lomond burial place of the MacGregors.

# MACINTYRE

**Chief of the Name and Arms:**
Donald Russell MacIntyre of Glenoe
**Motto:** 'Through hardship' ('*Per ardua*')
**Plant Badge:** White heather
www.macintyreclan.org

The 'Children of the Carpenter' who came
originally from the Hebrides to settle at Glen Noe
on the east side of Loch Etive in Argyll. Tradition
has it that it was an ancestor who secured the
marriage of Somerled to the King of Norway's
daughter Ragnhilda.

At some stage the MacIntyres acquired a
feudal obligation to the Campbells of Breadalbane which
entailed the presentation of a snowball in midsummer. Members
of the clan also served as hereditary foresters to the Lords of
Lorne and hereditary pipers to the Chiefs of Clan Menzies and
Clanranald. The MacIntyres did not take part in the Jacobite
Rising of 1745 when the chief was otherwise dissuaded by his
wife who was a Campbell.

In 1806, the chief and his family emigrated to the United
States of America. In 1991, the Coat of Arms of James Wallace
MacIntyre of Glenoe was confirmed by the Lord Lyon King of
Arms.

**ANCESTRAL INTEREST**

Sorn Castle, Ayrshire, KA5 6HR. Dates from 15th century and was remodelled by David Bryce in the 1860s. Originally owned by the Somervell family, the Sorn estate was purchased by Thomas MacIntyre in 1908. Gordon MacIntyre became a Senator of the College of Justice and took the judicial title of Lord Sorn. It remains a family home.

# MACKAY

**Chief of the Name and Arms:**
Aenes Simon Mackay, 15th Lord Reay
**Motto:** 'With a strong hand' (*Manu forti*)
**Plant Badge:** Bulrush
www.clanmackaysociety.co.uk

The Mackays claim descent from the Celtic Royal
House of Moray through the line of Morgund of
Pluscarden. In the 12th century, Mackay clansfolk
were dispersed to Sutherland by Malcolm IV
where their territories consisted of Farr, Tongue,
Durness and Edrahills, collectively known as
Strathnaver, and Reay in Caithness.

The clan supported Robert the Bruce at the Battle of
Bannockburn in 1314. In 1370, the Chief of Mackay of
Strathnaver and his son were murdered at Dingwall Castle by
Nicholas Sutherland of Duffus. Much bloodshed took place
between the Mackays and the Sutherlands, lasting through the
centuries.

In 1627, Sir Donald Mackay was created a Baronet of Nova
Scotia and the following year was elevated to the British Peerage
as Lord Reay. He was a staunch supporter of Charles I during the
English Civil War and went into exile in Denmark after the King
was executed. The Mackay clan took the side of the British
Government during the Jacobite Risings of 1715 and 1745.

MACKAY ANCIENT

## ANCESTRAL INTEREST

Eddrachilles on Badcall Bay, Scourie, IV27 4TH. Held by
Mackays from 1515–1757. Scourie, a crofting village, lies
within Eddrachilles estate.

Strathnaver Museum, Bettyhill, KW14 7SS. Opened in 1976. It
tells the history of the Mackays through to the Highland
Clearances.

Tongue House, Lairg, IV27 4XH. Former seat of Clan Mackay
from 1678 but acquired by the Sutherlands.

# MACKENZIE

**Chief of the Name and Arms**
John Grant Mackenzie, 5th Earl of Cromartie
**Motto:** 'I shine not burn' ('*Luceo non uro*')
**Plant Badge:** Deergrass
www.clanmackenziesociety.co.uk

 Clan Mackenzie territory stretched from their origins in Kintail to eventually envelope the Ross-shire landscape and the Isle of Lewis. Sharing a common ancestry from Gilleoin of the Aird, Celtic ruler of southern Ross, with Clan Anrias and Clan Matheson, the Mackenzies settled at Eilean Donan at the mouth of Loch Duich, where they were joined by the MacRaes who were appointed their hereditary standard bearers.

The Battle of Largs in 1263 terminated the power of the Norsemen of the west of Scotland and the Mackenzies earned the right to be part of the royal bodyguard, an honour kept until the death of James IV at the Battle of Flodden. The Mackenzies supported the Jacobite cause in the Risings of 1715 and 1745.

Kenneth Mackenzie of Kintail was created Lord Mackenzie of Kintail in 1609, and his eldest son was created Earl of Seaforth in 1623. His brother, Sir Ruaridh Mackenzie of Castle Leod and Tarbat, is the ancestor of the earls of Cromartie. The Seaforth line of Mackenzies died out in 1815. Tenants of the Seaforth estates were evicted by the trustees but were taken in by the Cromartie Mackenzies. In 1979, the 4th Earl of Cromartie was recognised as Chief of the Name by the Lord Lyon King of Arms.

MACKENZIE MODERN

**ANCESTRAL INTEREST**

Castle Leod, Strathpeffer, IV14 9AA. Seat of Clan Mackenzie.
   Home of the earls of Cromartie.

Chanonry Point, Black Isle, IV11. Memorial to Kenneth
   Mackenzie of Kintain, the Brahan Seer who prophesied the
   end of the Seaforth line.

Eilean Donan Castle, Kyle of Lochalsh, IV40 8DX. Thirteenth-
   century Mackenzie stronghold. Headquarters of Clan
   Mackenzie in the 12th century. Owned by the Conchra
   Charitable Trust.

# MACKINNON

**Chief of the Name and Arms:**
Madam Anne MacKinnon of MacKinnon
**Motto**: 'Fortune favours the bold' (*Audentes fortuna juvat*)
**Plant Badge**: Scots pine
www.themackinnon.com

Clan Mackinnon belonged to the kindred of St Columba. A branch of the seven clans of Sol Alpin from Fingon, great-grandson of King Kenneth MacAlpine, the clan is closely associated with the isles of Skye and Mull.

The Mackinnons gave shelter to Robert the Bruce when he was a fugitive and were rewarded with land on the Isle of Skye where they served as vassals to the Lord of the Isles and were at times 'Masters of the Household' and 'Marshals of the Army'. For many generations a branch held the post of hereditary standard bearer to the MacDonalds of Sleat. From 1467–1498, John Mackinnon was the last Benedictine Abbot of Iona.

The Mackinnons supported the Jacobite cause in the 17th and 18th century and the Chief of Mackinnon assisted in the escape of Prince Charles Edward Stuart to France after his defeat at the Battle of Culloden in 1746. For this, clan lands were confiscated. However, tradition has it that Prince Charles Edward handed the chief the recipe for Drambuie liqueur, which has been kept in the family ever since.

MACKINNON ANCIENT

## ANCESTRAL INTEREST

Dunakin Castle (Castle Maol), Kyleakin, Isle of Skye, IV41 8PL.
Ruined former seat of the Mackinnon Chiefs.

Mackinnon's Cave, Ardmeanach Peninsula, Isle of Mull. Only
accessible at low tide. The name was taken from a piper who
undertook to lead a party through the cave, but who
disappeared. However, his dog reappeared hairless with fright
on a clifftop some distance away.

# MACKINTOSH

**Chief of the Name and Arms:** John Mackintosh of Mackintosh
**Motto:** 'Touch not the cat bot a glove'
**Plant Badge:** Boxwood or red whortleberry
www.cmna.org; www.clanchattan.org.uk

The name Mackintosh means 'son of the thane'. Traditionally the founder is identified as the son of MacDuff of the Royal House of Dalriada, ancestor of the earls of Fife. In 1263, Ferquhar Mackintosh led the clan for Alexander II against the invasion of Haakon IV of Norway.

In 1291, Angus Mackintosh married Eva, daughter of the Chief of Clan Chattan. Clan Chattan subsequently developed into a remarkable confederation of independent clans, led by the Mackintosh Chief. During the Wars of Scottish independence, Clan Mackintosh supported Robert the Bruce.

The Battle of Palm Sunday between Clan Cameron and Clan Chattan took place in 1429. The clan supported the Marquis of Montrose and Charles I, and fought for the Jacobites in 1715 and 1745, suffering heavy losses at the Battle of Culloden in 1746. Following Culloden, Captain William McIntosh, an officer in the British Army, was sent to America where he married Senoya, a princess of the Wind Clan of the Creek Nation.

**ANCESTRAL INTEREST**

Moy Hall, Tomatin, IV13 7YQ. The present Moy Hall dates
from the 1950s to replace an original building, which dated
from c.1700, and the original Moy Castle which stood on an
island in Loch Moy. Charles Edward Stuart was entertained
here in 1746. It remains the seat of the Chief of Clan
Mackintosh.

Petty St Columba's Parish Church and Mackintosh Vault,
Inverness, IV2 7JJ. Burial place of the lairds of Mackintosh.

# MACLACHLAN (MACLAUGHLAN)

**Chief of the Name and Arms:** Euan John Maclachlan of Maclachlan, 25th of Maclachlan and Baron of Strathlachlan
**Motto:** 'Strong and faithful' (*Fortis et fidus*)
**Plant Badge:** Rowan
www.clan-maclachlan.org.uk; www.oldcastlelachlan.com

Also known as Clan Lachlan, this family is descended from Niall of the Nine Hostages, High King of Ireland. The Maclachlans originally held lands in Lochaber but through marriage acquired properties in Cowal.

The clan was a staunch supporter of the Royal House of Stuart. Lachlan of that Ilk accompanied the Earl of Mar at the Battle of Sheriffmuir in 1715, and the 17th Chief was killed fighting for the Jacobites at the Battle of Culloden in 1746. In Edinburgh, the Maclachlan colours were burned on the orders of the Duke of Cumberland.

In 1747, Donald Maclachlan of that Ilk received a charter for his lands 'at the intercession of the Duke of Argyll'. The Lachlan Trust is a registered Scottish Charity which takes donations to preserve the heritage of Clan Maclachlan. The Clan Maclachlan Society has branches in Australia, Great Britain and Ireland, Canada, New Zealand and the USA.

MACLACHLAN MODERN

**ANCESTRAL INTEREST**

Castle Lachlan, Strachur, Argyll, PA27 8BU. Ruins of old Castle
Lachlan on the shores of Loch Fyne, dating from 12th to 15th
century. New Castle Lachlan, a baronial mansion, was built
in 1790 by Donald, 19th Laird, and remodelled around 1910
by the architect George Mackie Watson.

Innis Chonnel Castle, Loch Awe, PA35 1HN. Also known as
Ardchonnel Castle. Ruins of old Campbell stronghold on an
island in Loch Awe where a cadet branch of the
MacLachlans were captains from 1613.

# MACLAINE OF LOCHBUIE
# (SEE ALSO MACLEAN)

**Chief of the Name and Arms:** The Much Honoured Lorne
Gillean Ian McLaine of Lochbuie, Baron of Moy
**Motto:** 'To conquer or die' (*Vincere vel mori*)
**Plant Badge**: Blackberry
www.maclaine.org

The MacLaines of Lochbuie are descended from
Hector Reaganach, brother of Lachlan Lubanach,
forebear of the MacLeans of Duart. The brothers
lived in the reign of Robert II in the 14th century.
The Chiefship was settled by tanistry (clan
assembly vote) whereby Duart was recognised as
Chief of Clan Maclean, although Hector was, in
fact, the older brother. Hector's son Charles was progenitor of
the Macleans of Glen Urquhart and Dochgarroch.

Charles, son of Hector, was granted lands on the Isle of Mull
by the Lords of the Isles around 1350 and had a seat on the
Council of the Isles, as did his successors until the forfeiture of
the Lordship in 1493. Murdoch Mor, 10th Chief of Lochbuie,
fought alongside the Marquis of Montrose in 1645. For this, his
lands were forfeit until they were restored to the family in 1661.

The MacLaines of Lochbuie were persuaded not to rise for
Prince Charles Edward Stuart in 1745 and therefore escaped the
repercussions that blighted the Highlands in the aftermath. John,
17th Chief of Lochbuie, was host to Dr Samuel Johnson and
James Boswell towards the end of their celebrated tour of the
Hebrides in 1773.

## ANCESTRAL INTEREST

Lochbuie House, Lochbuie, PA62 6AA. Built for John, 17th
  Laird of Lochbuie, and Murdoch, 19th of Lochbuie. In 1920,
  the Lochbuie estate was lost by the family in a law suit.

Moy Castle, Lochbuie, PA62 6AA. Ruins on Isle of Mull.
  Abandoned in 1752.

# MACLAREN
# (CLAN LABHRUINN)

**Chief of the Name and Arms**
Donald MacLaren of MacLaren and Achieskine
**Motto:** 'The boar's rock' (*'Creag an tuirc'*)
**Plant Badge:** Laurel
www.clanmaclarensociety.com; www.clanmaclarenna.org

MacLaren country encompassed Balquhidder on the banks of Loch Voil and the villages of Lochearnhead and Strathyre. A branch of the same origin occupied the Isle of Tiree, but descended from Fergus Mór mac Eirc, founder of the Kingdom of Dalriada in the 6th century. Maclaren chiefs were Hereditary Celtic Abbots of Achtow in Balquhidder.

The clan supported the Jacobite cause under Viscount Dundee at the Battle of Killiecrankie, and took part in the Risings of 1715 and 1745, culminating in defeat at the Battle of Culloden in 1746. Donald MacLaren was taken captive but escaped from prison in Carlisle, thereafter remaining a fugitive until the amnesty of 1757. The MacLarens continued to farm at Achtow until 1892, but with the clan largely dispersed, large numbers having emigrated to Canada and Australia.

In 1957, Donald MacLaren of MacLaren and Achleskine purchased land in Balquhidder in Stirlingshire and successfully matriculated his Arms at the Court of the Lord Lyon King of Arms. He was succeeded by his son in 1966.

MACLAREN MODERN

## ANCESTRAL INTEREST

Achleskine, Stirlingshire, FK19 8NZ. MacLaren clan heartland.
Creag an Tuirc, 'The Boar's Rock', Balquhidder, Stirlingshire,
    FK19 8PA. Ancient rallying point for Clan MacLaren.

# MACLEAN

**Chief of the Name and Arms:**
Sir Lachlan Hector Maclean of Duart and Morvern Bt
**Motto:** 'Virtue mine honour'
**Plant Badge:** Crowberry or holly
www.maclean.org

The Macleans descend from Gillean of the Battle Axe, who fought with Alexander II against the Norse invasion of Scotland at the Battle of Largs in 1263. He is acknowledged as belonging to the ancient Royal House of Lorn. Through subsequent service to the Lords of the Isles, the Macleans were rewarded with lands on the Isle of Mull, and through marriages with Clan Donald in the 13th century, the Bruces in the 14th century and Clan Mackenzie in the 15th century, consolidated their influence in the Hebrides.

By 1493, when the Lordship of the Isles was forfeited by Clan Donald, the Macleans held extensive island estates on Mull, Tiree, Islay and Jura, and Morvern, Lochaber and Knapdale on the Scottish mainland. These were divided between the four branches of Duart, Ardgour, Coll and Lochbuie.

Lachlan Maclean of Duart was killed fighting against the English with James IV at the Battle of Flodden in 1513. His descendant Sir Lachlan Maclean was a devoted Royalist and in 1647 the Maclean fortress of Duart was attacked by Government troops, and again by Clan Campbell in 1678. Clan Maclean supported the Jacobite cause in the Risings of 1689, 1715 and 1745.

## ANCESTRAL INTEREST

Aros Castle, Isle of Mull, PA72 6JP. Held by the Macleans in the 17th century. Now a ruin.

MACLEAN OF DUART HUNTING MODERN

Breachacha Castle, Isle of Coll, PA78 6TB. Seized by Maclean of
    Coll in 1431 but taken by Macleans of Duart after an inter-
    clan feud of 1578.

Duart Castle, Isle of Mull, PA64 6AP. Ancient clan seat guarding
    the Sound of Mull. Abandoned after the Jacobite Rising of
    1745, it was retrieved in 1911 by Sir Fitzroy Maclean, 10th
    Baronet and Chief of Clan Maclean. It is the home of the
    current chief and a great deal of restoration work has taken
    place, largely funded by clan supporters. The castle is open
    to the public during the summer months.

New Brachacha Castle, Isle of Coll, PA78 6TB. Built in 1750
    when the old castle (Historic Environment Scotland)
    became ruinous.

# MACLEOD

**Chief of the Name and Arms:**
Hugh Magnus MacLeod of MacLeod
**Motto:** 'Hold fast'
**Plant Badge:** Juniper
www.clanmacleod.org

Clan Macleod descends from Leod, son of Olaf the Black who lived in the early 13th century and was one of the last Norse kings of the Isle of Man and of the Isles of the North. Tradition has it that Leod inherited the Isle of Lewis and part of Skye from his brother and in c.1220 married the daughter of Paul Balkasson, the Norse Sheriff of Skye. Thus the MacLeods acquired Dunvegan Castle on the west coast of Skye. After his defeat at the Battle of Largs in 1263, King Haakon of Norway was forced to resign his residual claims to the Western Isles, leaving Leod in possession of almost half his former territories.

Leod had four sons. The eldest son, Tormod, inherited Dunvegan on Skye and the Isle of Harris, becoming chief of these lands and adopting the title MacLeod of Dunvegan. Leod's second son, Torquil, inherited the Isle of Lewis (Siol Torquil), but latterly descent in the male line failed and this distinction passed to MacLeod of Raasay.

The MacLeods paid rent to the Scottish Crowns from 1498 with three birlinns or war galleys held for the service of the King, plus a regular supply of peregrine falcons. The MacLeods supported the Royal Stuart dynasty during the War of the Three Kingdoms and lost 800 clansmen at the Battle of Worcester. As a result, they did not come out for the 1715 and 1745 Jacobite Risings. The impact of the subsequent potato famine in the Highlands bankrupted the Chief and it was only in 1929 that the 27th Chief of MacLeod took up residence at Dunvegan.

## ANCESTRAL INTEREST

Ardvreck Castle, Assynt, IV27 4HL. Built in 1591 by MacLeod of Assynt. Ruined site of the capture of the Marquis of Montrose in 1650.

Boreraig, Dunvegan Head, Isle of Skye, IV49 8ZY. Site of the MacCrimmon Memorial Cairn. The MacCrimmons were hereditary pipers to MacLeods for ten generations.

Dunvegan Castle, Isle of Skye, IV55 8WF. Hebridean stronghold dating from 13th century and home of the Chiefs of Clan MacLeod.

St Clement's Church and burial ground, Rodel, Isle of Harris, HS5 3TW. Several MacLeod of Harris chiefs are buried here.

# MACMILLAN

**Chief of the Name and Arms:**
Gordon MacMillan of MacMillan and Knap
**Motto:** 'I learn to succour the unfortunate'
('*Miseris succurrere disco*')
**Plant Badge:** Holly
www.clanmacmillan.org

A tribe of Moray who derived from the ancient Celtic tribe of Kanteai, one of the surviving clans of the Northern Picts. Historically, the Macmillans held lands on Tayside and supported the cause of Robert the Bruce, sheltering him at Lawers, east of Killin on the north side of Loch Tay. By 1360, Malcolm Mor Macmillan was established in Knapdale with a charter from the Lord of the Isles. However, most of these lands were lost by the 15th century and the Macmillans spread from Knapdale into Kintyre, Galloway and Kirkcudbright.

In 1742, the chiefship passed to Macmillan of Dunmore whose lands sat on the side of Loch Tarbert. Macmillan of Murlaggan refused to support the Jacobite cause unless Prince Charles Edward renounced the Catholic faith. However, two of his sons fought for the Prince and died at the Battle of Culloden in 1746. Hugh Macmillan, having survived the battle, guided the Prince on his escape route from Fasnakyle at the mouth of Glen Afric.

In the 20th century, General Sir Gordon Macmillan matriculated his arms when he was appointed Governor of Edinburgh Castle and, having married the granddaughter of George Jardine Kidston, established the seat of the Macmillan chiefs at Finlaystone House in Renfrewshire.

MACMILLAN HUNTING ANCIENT

### ANCESTRAL INTEREST

Castle Sween, Lochgilphead, PA31 8PT. Ruined courtyard castle
and former seat of Clan Macmillan. The castle passed to
Clan Campbell and is now in the care of Historic
Environment Scotland.

Finlaystone House, Renfrewshire, PA14 6TJ. Acquired by
General Sir Gordon Macmillan in the 20th century. Privately
owned.

# MACNAB

**Chief of the Name and Arms:** James Macnab of Macnab
**Motto:** 'Let fear be far from all' (*Timor omnis abesto*)
**Plant Badge:** Stone bramble
www.clanmacnabsociety.com

The Macnab surname translates as 'Child of the Abbot', and the ancestor of this clan is traditionally the Abbot of Glen Dochart and Strathearn, a younger son of King Kenneth MacAlpine. In the 12th century, Angus de Glendochart was married to the sister of John Comyn, rival to Robert the Bruce in his claim to the Scottish throne. When Bruce's power was consolidated in 1314, the Macnab lands were forfeited. However, Angus's grandson Gilbert was reinstated by David II in 1336.

Robert, 14th Chief of Macnab, was married to the sister of the Earl of Breadalbane and was therefore restricted from supporting the Jacobite Rising of 1715. The 15th Chief, a soldier in the Hanoverian army, was taken prisoner by Jacobites after the Battle of Prestonpans in 1745.

Francis, 16th Chief, was allegedly father of 32 children. According to a contemporary account, he 'produced the best whisky to be found in Scotland'. His successor Archibald was obliged to sell the clan lands to pay off debts and emigrated to Canada. He died in France in 1860 when it was established that the Arthurstone branch of the family should succeed. In 1954 the chiefship passed to Archibald Macnab who had re-purchased the Killin estate.

MACNAB MODERN

**ANCESTRAL INTEREST**

Innes Buidhe, Killin, FK21 8XE. Clan Macnab ancestral burial grounds.

Kinnell House, Killin, FK21 8SR. Built around 1590 and became ancestral home of the Macnab chiefs from 1654. Sold, bought back by 22nd Chief and then sold again in 1978 to cover death duties.

Sir Henry Raeburn's magnificent portrait 'The Macnab, 16th Chief', is on loan to the Kelvingrove Galleries in Glasgow.

# MACNA(U)GHTAN

**Chief of the Name and Arms:**
Sir Malcolm Francis MacNaghten of MacNaghten
**Motto:** 'I hope in God'
**Plant Badge:** Trailing azalea
www.clanmacnaughton.net

This clan claims descent from the ancient Mormaer of Moray. In 1267, Gilchrist MacNachtan was installed as keeper of the medieval royal castle of Fraoch Eilean on Loch Awe in Argyll by Alexander III.

The Macnaughtons initially joined Clan MacDougall in opposing Robert the Bruce in 1306. However, they later changed sides and fought with Robert the Bruce at the Battle of Bannockburn in 1314. In 1478, Alexander Macnaghtan received a charter for his lands from the Earl of Argyll, and his grandson was knighted for his services by James IV. He was one of the few survivors of the Battle of Flodden in 1513.

The Macnaghtans fought for the Jacobites at the Battle of Killiecrankie in 1689 and their lands were forfeited. In 1700, MacNaughton of Dunderave was married while under the influence of alcohol to the wrong daughter of Sir James Campbell of Ardkinglas. On discovering his mistake in the morning, he fled to Ireland with the younger sister, leaving his wife pregnant. The MacNaughton line continued in Antrim, Northern Ireland.

## ANCESTRAL INTEREST

Dunderave Castle, Inveraray, PA32 8XQ. Clan Macna(u)ghtan stronghold from the 15th century. Passed to Clan Campbell around 1689. Restored by the Noble family and still occupied.

Loch Dubh Castle, Glen Shira, Argyll, PA31 8SD. This castle was abandoned following an outbreak of plague. Only a mound remains.

# MACNEACAILL (NICOLSON)

**Chief of the Name and Arms:**
John MacNeacail of MacNeacail and Scorrybreac
**Motto:** '*Scorrybreac*'
**Plant Badge:** Juniper
www.clanmacnicol.org; www.clanmacnicol.com

This surname is shared by two interlinked Scottish families, the Lowland Clan Nicolson and the unrelated Clan MacNeacail of Skye. The Nicolson surname is thought to have come about when the Highland clan decided to Anglicise its Gaelic name.

Prince Charles Edward Stuart sheltered in the byre at Scorrybreac as a fugitive in 1746. In the 19th century, the Highland clan was badly disrupted by the Highland Clearances and the chief was forced to abandon Scorrybreac and emigrate to Tasmania. Sheriff Alasdair Nicolson was a member of the Napier Commission that brought about the Crofters Act of 1886.

The chiefly line claims descent from James Nicolson, an Edinburgh lawyer who died c.1580, and whose ancestors had been burgesses of Aberdeen in the 15th century. His eldest son, John, acquired lands in Lasswade while his younger son James entered the Church and was appointed Bishop of Dunkeld. John's son was created a Baronet of Nova Scotia as Nicolson of that Ilk in 1629. The direct male line died out in 1826. In 1984, the Name and Arms of Nicolson were confirmed by the Lord Lyon King of Arms on Adam Nicholson, 5th Baron Carnock. Lyon also granted a petition to Ian Nicolson of Scorrybreac of the West Highland clan to be recognised as Chief of MacNeacall in his own right.

## ANCESTRAL INTEREST

Castle MacNicol, Stornoway, Isle of Lewis, HS2 0XR. Original
   stronghold of Clan MacNeacaill from 1100. Destroyed
   during Oliver Cromwell's invasion of Scotland in the 17th
   century and its remains were used to build foundations for
   the Stornoway pier in 1852.

Scorrybreac House (Ben Torvaig), Portree, Isle of Skye,
   IV51 9DH. Stronghold of Clan MacNeacaill for over 800
   years but fell into ruin and was demolished. A monument
   was raised by Dr J.G. Nicholson on the site.

# MACNEIL (CLAN NIALL)

**Chief of the Name and Arms:** Roderick MacNeil of Barra
**Motto:** 'Conquer or die' (*'Buaidh no bas'*)
**Plant Badge:** Dryas
www.clanmacneilglobal.org

The MacNeil clan takes its surname from Niall of the Nine Hostages, High King of Ireland, whose descendant came to the island of Barra in c.1049. In 1427, Gilleonan Roderick Murchaid Macneil received a charter for Barra and Boisdale from the Lords of the Isles. The 12th Chief was tricked into attending James V at Portree and arrested and held prisoner until 1542. The 15th Chief was known as 'Ruari the Turbulent' for being so troublesome.

In 1688, his great-grandson Roderick Dhu received a Crown charter 'for all the lands of Barra'. The MacNeills were Jacobites and Roderick Dhu fought at the Battle of Killiecrankie in 1689 and rallied to the cause in 1715. His two sons were forced into exile but, despite this, the estates were not forfeit.

The clan prospered until 1838 when the 21st Chief was forced to sell Barra and the Chiefship passed to a branch of the family which had emigrated to America. In 1937, the American cousins returned to reclaim the Kisimul estate, restoring the castle for Clan MacNeil.

MACNEIL OF BARRA MODERN

## ANCESTRAL INTEREST

Castle Sween, Lochgilphead, PA31 8PT. Twelfth-century Norman keep. Historic Environment Scotland. The MacNeills of Gigha were appointed hereditary keepers in the 15th century.

Kisimul Castle, Castle Bay, Isle of Barra, HS9 5UZ. Thirteenth-century castle, although the tower possibly dates from 1120. The semi-ruined castle was restored in the 20th century by Robert Lister MacNeil. In 2001 it was leased to Historic Environment Scotland for 1,000 years for the annual sum of £1 and a bottle of Scotch whisky.

Weaver's Castle, Eilean Leathan, Stack Islands off Isle of Eriskay, Outer Hebrides. Ruins of a lair used by the MacNeil pirate wreckers.

# MACPHERSON

**Chief of the Name and Arms:**
James Brodie Macpherson of Cluny, 7th of Blairgowrie
**Motto:** 'Touch not the cat bot a glove'
**Plant Badge:** White heather
www.clan-macpherson.org

The Clan Macpherson derives its surname from the Gaelic Mac a' Phearsein, which means 'son of the parson'. Marriage was allowed in the Celtic Church, and the recognised ancestor of this clan is Muireach, or Murdo, Cattenach, Priest of Kingussie in Badenoch. The Macphersons became an integral part of the mighty Clan Chattan Federation which comprised twelve separate Highland clans.

Clan tradition is that the lands of Badenoch were gifted to the Chief of Macpherson by Robert the Bruce in 1309. The clan is sometimes known as the Clan of the Three Brothers from the sons of Ewan Ban Macpherson: Macpherson of Cluny, Macpherson of Pitman and Macpherson of Invershie. In 1370 a raiding party of Camerons was confronted by the Macphersons, Mackintoshes and Davidsons at Invernahavon. The feud between the Camerons and Clan Chattan continued until brought to a head in the presence of Robert III at the Battle of the North Inch in Perth.

In the Jacobite Rising of 1745, Macpherson of Cluny transferred his loyalties to Prince Charles Edward Stuart and, following the Battle of Culloden in 1746, for nine years dodged capture by the government troops who sought to arrest him. The Cluny estate was forfeited but returned in 1784. Several acres at Newtonmore are used for the annual Newtonmore Highland Games.

MACPHERSON RED ANCIENT

## ANCESTRAL INTEREST

Balavil, Kingussie, PH21 1LU. Home of James ('Ossian')
    Macpherson (1736–96). Privately owned.
Ballindalloch Castle, Banffshire, AB37 9AX. Built by Clan Grant
    before marriage to the Macphersons. Owned by
    Macpherson-Grant family.
Clan Macpherson Museum, Newtonmore, PH20 1DE. Entry is
    free.
Cluny Castle, Laggan, Newtonmore, PH20 1BS. Original castle
    dated from 14th century but destroyed after the 1745 Jacobite
    Rising. Privately owned.
Newton Castle, Blairgowrie, Perthshire, PH10 6SU. Seat of
    Macpherson Chiefs.

# MACTAVISH

**Chief of the Name and Arms:**
Steven Dugald MacTavish of Dunardry
**Motto:** 'Not forgotten' ('*Non oblitus*')
www.clanmactavish.org

The chiefly line of MacTavish is styled MacTavish of Dunardry, strongly associated by some with Clan Campbell, but otherwise connected with an Irish/Pictish origin.

The 6th Chief of MacTavish, along with his son and heir and brother, lost their lives fighting for James IV against the English army at the Battle of Flodden in 1513. The MacTavishes are believed to have supported the Jacobite cause but initially took no action because of their Campbell neighbours who supported the Government. In 1745, Chief Archibald and his son were imprisoned for suspected treason at Dumbarton Castle, although some of their clansmen fought in the Jacobite army with Clan Mackintosh.

The Dunardry estate was sold by public auction in 1785. Twelve years later it was purchased by the wealthy Simon MacTavish of Montreal, from the Garthbeg branch of the Clan. In 1997, Edward Dugald MacTavish, great-grandson of William MacTavish of the Hudson's Bay Company and Governor of Manitoba, was granted the Arms and Title of Chief of Clan MacTavish of Dunardry by the Lord Lyon King of Arms.

**ANCESTRAL INTEREST**

Dunardry Castle, Knapdale, Argyll. Ancient site occupied by the
   MacTavishes but destroyed to make way for the Crinan
   Canal.
Kilchrist Castle, Machrihanish, Argyll, PA28 6PH. Medieval
   castle rebuilt by Dugald MacTavish in 1834. Privately owned.

# MACTHOMAS

**Chief of the Name and Arms:**
Andrew MacThomas of Finegand
**Motto:** 'God help overcome envy'
(*Deo juvante invidiam superabo*)
www.clanmacthomas.uk

Tomaidh Mor, a Gaelic-speaking Highlander also known as 'Great Tommy', was a grandson of William Mackintosh, 7th Chief of Mackintosh and 8th Chief of Clan Chattan. He lived in the 15th century. When the Clan Chattan Federation became large and unmanageable, he took his kinsmen and followers across the Grampian Mountains to Badenoch and Glenshee.

Early MacThomas chiefs settled at the Thom on the east coast of the Shee Water, opposite the Spittal of Glenshee. Ian Mor, 7th Chief of MacThomas, joined the Royalist army of the Marquis of Montrose at Dundee in 1644 but withdrew after the Battle of Philiphaugh in 1645. Following the Restoration, MacThomas was fined heavily and the Earl of Airlie attempted to seize some of his lands. The clan scattered after his death.

However, the chiefly line became successful farmers in Fife, before moving to Dundee. The 16th Chief became Provost of Dundee in 1847. In 1954, the Clan MacThomas Society was founded by Patrick, 18th Chief of MacThomas.

MACTHOMAS MODERN

## ANCESTRAL INTEREST

Finegand, Perth and Kinross. A farming hamlet on the Shee Water once occupied by Clan MacThomas.

Forter Castle, Kirkton of Glenisla, PH11 8QW. Built in 1560 by James Ogilvy, 5th Lord Airlie. Burned by Clan Campbell but Barony purchased by Iain McComie Mor in 17th century. Rebuilt in the 1990s and privately owned.

McComie Mor's Putting Stone, McComie Mor's Chair and McComie Mor's Well are located in Glen Prosen, north of Kirriemuir. The MacThomas Gathering Ground is located at the Thom, opposite the Spittal of Glenshee.

# MALCOLM (MACCALLUM)

**Chief of the Name and Arms:**
Robin Neill Malcolm, 19th Laird of Poltalloch
**Motto:** 'He aims at difficult things' (*In ardua tendit*)
**Plant Badge:** Mountain ash
www.clan-maccallum-malcolm.org/

The surname is derived from Mac Ghillie Chaluim, 'Son of the disciple of St Columba'. Although it appears in the 14th century and is the Christian name of four Scottish kings, the clan surname of Malcolm was only adopted in the 18th century when the Chief of Clan MacCallum inherited the Malcolm estates in 1779.

It is known that the MacCallums were settled in Lorn in the late 13th century, but the first appearance of note is in 1414 when Ronald MacCallum is listed as constable of Craignish Castle. A century later, Donald Gillespie O'Challum was given a charter from Campbell of Duntrune for the lands of Poltalloch at Kilmartin in Argyll.

John Wingfield Malcolm of Poltalloch had a distinguished parliamentary career and was created Lord Malcolm of Poltalloch in 1896. Both he and the title died without heir in 1902, and he was succeeded as Chief of Clan Malcolm by his brother Edward. Edward's son Sir Iain, a director of the Suez Canal Company, was made Knight of the Order of St Michael and St George and awarded the Légion d'Honneur by France.

MALCOLM ANCIENT

## ANCESTRAL INTEREST

Duntrune Castle, Argyll, PA31 8QQ. Originally built for Clan
    MacDougall but sold to the Malcolms of Poltalloch in 1792.
    The estate remains in the ownership of the Malcolm Chief.
Lochore Castle, Lochgelly, Fife, KY5 8AF. Ruined 14th-century
    fortress which was occupied by Malcolms of Balbedie in the
    17th century.
Poltalloch, Kilmartin, PA31 8QF. Ruin of Victorian Jacobean
    mansion designed by William Burn.

# MAR

**Chief of the Name and Arms:**
Margaret of Mar, 31st Countess of Mar
**Motto:** 'Think more' (*Pans plus*)
www.tribeofmar.com

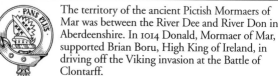

The territory of the ancient Pictish Mormaers of Mar was between the River Dee and River Don in Aberdeenshire. In 1014 Donald, Mormaer of Mar, supported Brian Boru, High King of Ireland, in driving off the Viking invasion at the Battle of Clontarff.

In 1248 William, 5th Earl of Mar, appears as one of the Regents of Scotland and Great Chamberlain of the Realm. The Mars supported Robert the Bruce's claim to the Scottish throne and the Chief's eldest daughter, Isabella, was Robert the Bruce's first wife. Her brother Gratney, 7th Earl of Mar, married Bruce's sister Christina. In 1332 Donald, 8th Earl, was chosen to become Regent of Scotland but died ten days later. The Celtic earldom then passed through the female line to Donald's daughter Margaret and granddaughter Isabella, whose second husband was Alexander Stewart, known as the Wolf of Badenoch.

On Isabella's death c.1407, the Mar earldom of the first creation passed to Robert, Lord Erskine, who was himself descended from Gratney. However, the rights to the earldom were subsequently claimed by James II, citing the Stewart marriage. In 1565 Mary, Queen of Scots restored the title to the Erskines. In 1715 the exiled James VIII created John Erskine Duke of Mar. When he was exiled for rebellion, all of the family honours were forfeited until the earldom of 1565 was restored to the Erskines by Charles II in 1824. Thereafter it becomes confusing, since there is now an earldom of Mar and an earldom of Mar and Kellie, the latter from 1565 and held by the Chief of Clan Erskine. This must

MARR GREEN MODERN

not be confused with the separate ancient earldom of the Chief of the Tribe of Mar.

**ANCESTRAL INTEREST**

Braemar Castle, Ballater; AB35 5XR. Constructed in 1628 for John Erskine, Earl of Mar. Attacked and burned by Farquharson of Inverey in 1689, Braemar Castle was garrisoned following the 1745 Jacobite Rising. Braemar Castle is run by Braemar Community Ltd and staffed by local volunteers.

Kildrummy Castle, Alford, AB33 8RA. Ancestral seat of earls of Mar. Ruin dating from 13th century. Historic Environment Scotland.

157

# MATHESON

**Chief of the Name and Arms:** Sir Alexander Matheson of
Matheson, 8th Baronet of Lochalsh
**Motto:** 'Do and hope' (*'Fac et spera'*)
**Plant Badge:** Broom
www.clanmatheson.org

The surname translates from the Gaelic as 'Son of
the Bear'. Descent is given from Kenneth
MacAlpine, King of Scots, and the clan is an early
offshoot of the Celtic earldom of Ross established
around Loch Alsh, Loch Carron and Kintail. A
branch of the clan settled in Sutherland.

Clan Matheson fought for the Lord of the
Isles at the Battle of Harlaw in 1411, and their fighting force was
then estimated at two thousand. However, with the collapse of
the Lordship of the Isles, Clan Matheson was caught up in the
ongoing feuds between Clan Donald and Clan Mackenzie.
Donald Matheson of Shin supported the Hanoverians during the
Rising of 1715, while his kinsman John Matheson fought
alongside the Jacobites at the Battle of Culloden in 1746.

Sir James Sutherland Matheson, born in Sutherland,
co-founded with William Jardine the Hong Kong-based trading
conglomerate Jardine, Matheson & Co in 1832 and amassed a
great family fortune.

MATHESON RED MODERN

## ANCESTRAL INTEREST

Ardross Castle, Alness, IV17 0YE. Originally owned by Clan
Munro but acquired in 1845 by Sir Alexander Matheson, a
scion of the Far Eastern Trading Company.

Fort Matheson, Balmacara, Kyle, IV40 8DH. Original seat of
Clan Matheson on Loch Achaidh na h-Inich but now only a
remnant remains.

Lews Castle, Stornoway, Isle of Lewis HS2 0XP. This was built by
the family of Sir James Matheson (1796–1878) who bought
the estate in 1846. It was previously known as Seaforth Lodge
and is now apartments and houses. Also the site of Museum
nan Eilean, with hotel accommodation and the Storehouse
cafe.

# MENZIES

**Chief of the Name and Arms:**
David Ronald Steuart Menzies of that Ilk
**Motto:** 'God willing I shall' (*'Vil God I Zal'*)
**Plant Badge:** The Menzies' heath
www.menzies.org

This is a Norman name derived from Mayneris, near Rouen in France. The earliest definitive chief was Sir Robert de Myneris who became Chamberlain of Scotland in 1249. Records of the early history of the Menzies clan were lost in a fire which destroyed the first castle at Weem in 1502.

However, extensive lands from Glendochart to Aberfeldy in Perthshire were granted to Sir Alexander Meygners, son of Sir Robert, for services to Robert the Bruce. King Robert later bestowed upon Sir Alexander the baronies of Glendochart and Durisdeer.

In later centuries, the principal Menzies territories became Weem, the Appin of Dull and Rannoch, and a branch of the family became established at Pitfodels in Aberdeenshire, Durisdeer in Nithsdale, Shian at Glenquaich, Culdares in Glenlyon, Rotmell in Dowally, Perthshire, Vogrie in Midlothian and Coulter in Lanarkshire.

The Menzies baronetcy came to an end with the death of Sir Neil Menzies of Menzies in 1910 and, following the death of his sister in 1918, the estates were sold. Castle Menzies was occupied by the Polish army during the Second World War and in 1957 was purchased and restored by the Menzies Clan Society.

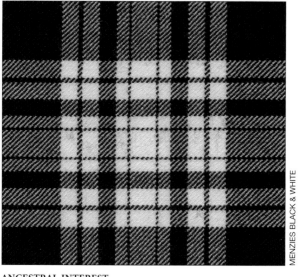

## ANCESTRAL INTEREST

Castle Menzies, Aberfeldy, PH15 2JD. Sixteenth-century seat of
    Clan Menzies for over 500 years. Open to the public.
    Menzies Charitable Trust.

Comrie Castle, Perthshire, PH15 2LS. Ruins of original seat of
    Clan Menzies on River Lyon. Last occupied in 1748.

Menzies Mausoleum, Old Kirk of Weem, Aberfeldy, PH15 2LD.

# MOFFAT

**Chief of the Name and Arms:** Jean Moffat of that Ilk
**Motto:** 'I hope for better things' (*Spero meliora*)
www.clanmoffat.org

A Borders family, almost certainly from Normandy, which rose to prominence at the time of Sir William Wallace and undoubtedly gave their name to the town of Moffat in Dumfries and Galloway. By the 12th century, the family were known as 'de Moffet'.

The Moffats were granted four charters of land in the barony of Westerkirk by Robert the Bruce, Lord of Annandale. Adam of Knock and his brother both fought alongside their clansmen for Robert the Bruce at the Battle of Bannockburn in 1314. Branches of the clan were to be found at Craigbeck and Garrowgill and Hawkshaw in Tweeddale. During the 16th century, in company with most of their neighbours, Clan Moffat turned to raiding and became established as Border Reivers, notably feuding with Clan Johnstone.

With the murder of Robert Moffat by Clan Johnstone in 1557, the clan remained leaderless until 1983 when Francis Moffat of that Ilk was recognised as hereditary chief by the Lord Lyon King of Arms.

MOFFAT ANCIENT

## ANCESTRAL INTEREST

Moffat, Dumfries and Galloway. Scottish Borders town on River Annan. The name originates from that of Clan Moffat who arrived in the vicinity in the 13th century. In 1342, they were granted the feu of Granton and Reddings by Sir John Douglas, Lord of Annandale.

# MONCREIFFE

**Chief of the Name and Arms:**
The Hon. Peregrine Moncreiffe of that Ilk
**Motto:** 'Upon hope' ('*Sur esperance*')
**Plant Badge:** Oak
www.moncreiffe.org

This surname is taken from the lands of
Moncreiffe which were gifted in 1248 to Sir
Matthew Moncreiffe, who also held lands in
Strathearn, Fife and Atholl. The tradition is that
Sir Matthew was descended from Maldred of
Dunkeld, brother of King Duncan I of Scotland.

In 1568, William Moncreiffe, 11th Chief of
Moncreiffe, entered into a treaty with 'the haill name of Murray'
for their mutual defence. Sir Thomas Moncreiffe was Clerk of
the Exchequer during the reigns of Charles II, James VII and
William and Mary. In 1663, Thomas Moncreiffe was created a
Baronet of Nova Scotia and purchased the Moncreiffe estate
from his cousin.

During the 20th century, Sir Iain Moncreiffe of that Ilk
inherited the baronetcy and lands of Moncreiffe from a kinsman
and served as Albany Herald at the Court of the Lord Lyon King
of Arms. In 1946, he married Lady Diana Hay, only child of the
22nd Earl of Erroll who, under the Celtic tradition of
inheritance, subsequently became Countess of Erroll in her own
right. On her death, the Erroll earldom passed to her eldest son.
On the death of Sir Iain, the Moncreiffe baronetcy passed to
their eldest son and the chiefship to their younger son.

MONCREIFFE MUTED

**ANCESTRAL INTEREST**

Moncreiffe House, Bridge of Earn, Perthshire, PH2 8PZ. Listed
building designed by Sir William Bruce of Kinross and
destroyed by a fire in 1957 when it claimed the life of the
10th Baronet. It was rebuilt to a design by Sir William
Kininmonth in 1962 and remains a private home. Lands held
by the Moncreiffe family since the 13th century.

# MONTGOMERY

**Chief:** The Rt Hon. Hugh Montgomerie,
19th Earl of Eglinton and 7th Earl of Winton
**Motto:** 'Watch well' ('*Garde bien*')
www.clanmontgomery.org

Roger de Montgomery held the Castle of Sainte-Foy-de-Montgommery near Lisieux in Normandy, and accompanied William the Conqueror to England in 1066. He afterwards captured territory in Wales, to which he gave his name. The first recorded Montgomery in Scotland was Robert de Montgomerie who was granted the lands of Eaglesham in Renfrewshire in the reign of David I. His descendant Sir John Montgomery, 7th Baron of Eaglesham, was one of the heroes of the Battle of Otterburn in 1388.

Sir Alexander Montgomery was created Lord Montgomery in 1449. Following the death of James IV at the Battle of Flodden in 1514, Hugh, 3rd Lord Montgomery, who had been created Earl of Eglinton in 1508, was nominated to become of the Queen Dowager's Counsellors. The 2nd Earl of Eglinton and his men fought for Mary, Queen of Scots at the Battle of Langside where he was taken prisoner and imprisoned but later released. His daughter married Robert Seton, 1st Earl of Winton. In 1840, the 13th Earl of Eglinton was served as heir to the 4th Earl of Winton.

It was the 13th Earl of Eglinton who in 1839 conceived the great and extremely extravagant tournament and pageant at Eglinton Castle, seeking to recapture the thrills of medieval jousting. On the day torrential rain made it a washout.

166

MONTGOMERY BLUE MODERN

**ANCESTRAL INTEREST**

Eglinton Castle, Kilwinning, KA13 7QA. Seat of the earls of
  Eglinton, the original fortress having been burned by the
  Earl of Glencairn in 1528. Rebuilt between 1797 and 1802.
  Debts and death duties led to it being abandoned and the
  roof removed in 1925.
Skelmorlie Castle, Largs, PA17 5EY. Former seat and stronghold
  of the Montgomery clan from 1502. Sold by 16th Earl of
  Eglinton in the mid-1970s. Today privately owned.

# MORRISON

**Chief of the Name and Arms:**
Dr John Ruairidh Morrison of Ruchdi
**Motto:** 'Pabbay family' (*Teaghlach Phabbay*)
**Plant Badge:** Driftweed
www.clanmorrison.net

Of Scandinavian origin, centred on the Isle of Lewis. There is an apocryphal tale of a natural son of a King of Norway who was cast ashore clinging to a piece of driftwood. Although the clan is thought to have established itself on the Isle of Mull, the Morrisons of Habost and Barvas held the hereditary brieveship (judge) of Lewis until 1613. For their various services, they were rewarded with lands around Ness. On his deathbed in the 16th century, Hutcheon Morrison confessed that he had fathered Torquil, assumed to be the son of the MacLeod Chief. Torquil was disinherited and immediately made an alliance with the hitherto peaceful Morrisons. However, this led to Clan Morrison being dispossessed of their lands. They were later returned to them but the Morrisons continued to be at odds with the MacLeods and their neighbours, the MacAulays of Uig.

The Morrison surname is also found on the mainland at Durness in Sutherland and in Perth, Stirling and Dumbarton. The senior line of the mainland clan was the Morrisons of Bognie in Aberdeenshire. However, their links with the west coast and Hebridean Morrisons remain uncertain.

Until the 20th century, the Morrisons of Bognie were considered to be the senior 'armigerous' Morrison clan. However, in 1965 the Lord Lyon King of Arms recognised John Morrison of Ruchdi as the 'principal chief of the whole name and clan of Morrison'.

MORRISON HUNTING ANCIENT

## ANCESTRAL INTEREST

Conzie Castle (also known as Bognie Castle), Huntly,
    AB54 6BW. Built by Clan Morrison in the 17th century.
Dùn Èistean, Knockaird, Isle of Lewis, HS2 0XF. Remains of
    Clan Morrison stronghold.

# MUNRO

**Chief of the Name and Arms:** Hector Munro of Foulis
**Motto:** 'Dread God'
**Plant Badge:** Club moss
www.clanmunro.org.uk

Historically based in Easter Ross, Clan Munro's founder Donald arrived in the 11th century from the north of Ireland to settle on lands granted by Malcolm II. Tradition has it that the clan under Robert Munro supported Robert the Bruce during the Wars of Scottish Independence, and by then held lands principally at Ferindonald on the Black Isle, but exchanged these in 1350 for Estirfowyls.

During the 15th and 16th centuries, the Munros fought for the Lord of the Isles at the Battle of Harlaw in 1411 and feuded with their neighbours, Clan Mackenzie of Kintail. In 1527, a bond of friendship was signed between Hector Munro of Foulis, John Campbell of Cawdor, Hector Mackintosh of Mackintosh, Hugh Rose of Kilravock and Donald of Sleat. A further bond of alliance was signed in 1544 between Hector Munro, 14th Baron of Foulis and the Chief of Clan Ross of Balnagowan.

Robert Munro, 15th Baron of Foulis, was a staunch supporter of Mary, Queen of Scots, fighting on her behalf at the siege of Inverness in 1562. In the 17th century, clan members supported the Covenanters and Royalists, and remained staunchly anti-Jacobite during the Risings of 1715 and 1745.

## ANCESTRAL INTEREST

Foulis Castle, Evanton, IV16 9UX. Ancestral seat of the chiefs of
  Clan Munro dating from the 12th century.

Fyrish Monument, Alness, IV16 9XL. Memorial to General
  Hector Munro (1726–1805) of nearby Novar House, based
  on the Gate of Negapatam, a port in Madras, India.

Novar House, Dingwall, IV169X. Eighteenth-century castle built
  on an earlier site. Created by Sir Hector Munro, 8th of
  Novar (1726–1805). Private home.

# MURRAY

**Chief of the Name and Arms:**
Bruce Murray, 12th Duke of Atholl
**Motto:** 'Quite ready' (*'Tout prest'*)
**Plant Badge:** Juniper
www.clanmurray.org

Freskin de Moravia of Duffus in Moray was a nobleman of Flemish descent and appears in the 12th century as Chieftain of the Duffus branch of the Royal House of Moray. He acquired lands from David I. His grandson married the heiress of Bothwell and Drumsgard in Lanarkshire, and Smailholm in Berwickshire. From their son descend the Murrays of Tullibardine, ancestors of the earls and dukes of Atholl.

Sir John Murray, 12th Feudal Baron of Tullibardine, was created Lord Murray of Tullibardine in 1604, then Earl of Tullibardine in 1606. William, 2nd Earl, rescued James VI at Perth in the Gowrie Conspiracy. He married Lady Dorothea Stewart, daughter of John, 5th Stewart Earl of Atholl, and the two earldoms merged in 1607. In 1676, the 2nd Murray Earl of Atholl and 5th Earl of Tullibardine was created Marquis of Atholl. The 2nd Marquis of Atholl was created Duke of Atholl in 1703. Lord George Murray was the Jacobite general who secured the early victories of the Rising of 1745 while his elder brother the Duke sided with the Hanoverian Government. In 1845, Queen Victoria presented colours to the Atholl Highlanders.

In 1600, Sir David Murray was granted the lands of Scone by James VI and was later created Viscount Stormont. His descendants became earls of Mansfield (Nottingham) and Mansfield (Middlesex). The earldom of Dunmore was created in 1886 for Lord Charles Murray, second son of the 1st Marquis of Atholl.

172

MURRAY OF ATHOLL MODERN

## ANCESTRAL INTEREST

Blair Castle, Pitlochry, PH18 5TL. Ancestral home of Clan
    Murray. Acquired from Comyns of Badenoch and Stewarts.
    It was occupied twice by the Jacobites during the Risings of
    1715 and 1745. Owned by a charitable trust.

Bothwell Castle, Uddingston, G71 8BL. Land acquired by Walter
    de Moravia in 1252. The castle passed to Clan Douglas after
    the Scottish Wars of Independence.

Duffus Castle, Lossiemouth, IV30 5RH. Built by Freskin de
    Moravia in c.1140. Historic Environment Scotland.

# NAPIER

**Chief of the Name and Arms:** The Rt Hon. Francis David Napier, 15th Lord Napier and 6th Baron Ettrick
**Motto:** 'Without stain' ('Sans tache')
**Plant Badge:** Heather
www.clannapier.org

The Napier surname was recorded in Scotland in 1140 but the heraldry of Napier of Merchiston indicates a descent from the Lennox Family, ancient Celtic Mormaers of Levenax. The Napiers of Napier in Renfrewshire claim this descent and their surname is said to derive from Alexander III's statement after a battle that 'Lennox has nae peer'. In other words: 'no equal'.

Alexander Napier and his grandson were killed fighting for James IV at the Battle of Flodden in 1513 and another Napier heir was killed at the Battle of Pinkie in 1547. Lord Napier, son of John Napier (1550–1617) was the inventor of logarithms. A descendant of Napier's married a sister of the Marquis of Montrose and as a Royalist was forced into exile. He died in the Netherlands in 1660.

After the 3rd Lord Napier died, the title passed to his sister and on to his nephew through a special arrangement. Robert Napier, born in Dumbarton in 1791, became a prominent Victorian shipbuilder on the River Clyde.

**ANCESTRAL INTEREST**

Kilmahew Castle, Cardross, G82 5NL. Ruins of castle built on
 land gifted to the Napiers by the Earl of Lennox c.1290.

Lauriston Castle, Edinburgh, EH4 6AD. A 16th-century tower
 house with 19th-century extensions overlooking the Firth of
 Forth. Rebuilt for a son of Sir Archibald Napier around 1590.
 The City of Edinburgh Council has administered the house
 as a museum since 1926.

Merchiston Tower, Edinburgh, EH10 5DT. Built in 1454, it
 became the home of John, 8th Laird of Merchiston, inventor
 of logarithms. Today it stands at the centre of Napier
 University's Merchiston campus.

# NESBITT

**Chief of the Name and Arms:** Mark Nesbitt of that Ilk
**Motto:** 'I byd it' ('I endure')
**Plant Badge:** Oak
www.nesbittnisbet.org.uk

The surname derives from the old Barony of Nesbit in Berwickshire and is first on record in the 12th century. Two signatories of the surname Nisbet appear on the Ragman Rolls of the 13th century. Thomas of Nesbitt served as Prior of Coldingham from 1219 to 1240.

Nesbitts supported the Royalist cause and joined King Charles I's standard at Oxford. Philip Nesbit was captured at the battle of Philiphaugh and executed in 1646. The distinguished heraldic writer Alexander Nisbet was his nephew. His great work *System of Heraldry* was first published in 1722.

In the 16th century, some members of the Nesbit/Nisbet family emigrated to Ireland and onwards to America while others moved to live in Sweden where their descendants can still be found.

NISBET MODERN

## ANCESTRAL INTEREST

Dirleton Castle, East Lothian, EH39 5ER. A medieval fortress originally built by the Norman family of de Vaux and purchased in 1663 by the lawyer John Nisbet, Lord Direlton, when already a ruin. He built nearby Archerfield House (now transformed into a hotel). His daughter Mary Hamilton Nesbit inherited a great fortune and married the 7th Earl of Elgin. It was her inherited wealth that funded the saving of the so-called Elgin Marbles from the Parthenon in Athens.

Nisbet Castle, Duns, TD11 3HU. A 17th-century mansion on Blackadder Water built c.1630 by Sir Alexander Nisbet. Sold to Clan Ker in 1653. Today private residence.

# OGILVY/OGILVIE

**Chief:** David Ogilvy, 13th Earl of Airlie
**Motto:** 'To the end' (*A fin*)
**Plant Badge:** Pentaglottis
www.clanogilvie.com

Gillebride, second son of Gilliechriost, Mormaer of Angus, received the barony of Ogilvy in the Parish of Glamis c.1163. In 1365, the Ogilvys were appointed Hereditary Sheriffs of Angus and in 1369 Sir Walter Ogilvy acquired the barony of Cortachy. Sir Walter Ogilvy, younger son of Ogilvy of Wester Powrie, was appointed Treasurer of Scotland in 1425. In 1430, he was Ambassador to England and had several sons, one of whom became ancestor to the earls of Seafield.

Sir James Ogilvy, having served as Scottish Ambassador to Denmark, was created Lord Ogilvy of Airlie in 1491. James, 7th Lord Ogilvy of Airlie, a devout Royalist, was created Earl of Airlie in 1639. Airlie lands included Glenisla, Glenprosen, and Glenclova in Angus. Through marriage into the Sinclair family, the Ogilvys also held the earldom of Findlater from 1638, a title which eventually passed to the Grant family.

The 2nd Earl was captured at the Battle of Philiphaugh in 1644. He was sentenced to death but escaped. The Ogilvys rallied to the Stuart cause in both the 1715 and 1745 Risings. As a consequence, their lands and titles were confiscated but restored in 1896 by an Act of Parliament.

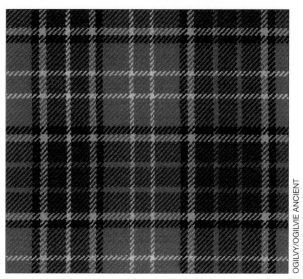

OGILVY/OGILVIE ANCIENT

## ANCESTRAL INTEREST

Airlie Castle, Kirriemuir, DD8 5NG. An Ogilvy stronghold from
  1430, but superseded by a mansion house in 1763.
Cortachy Castle, Kirriemuir, DD8 4LX. Held by the Ogilvys of
  Airlie since the 17th century.
Winton Castle, East Lothian, EH34 5AT. Masterpiece of Scottish
  Renaissance architecture. Passed from the Seton earls of
  Winton through the Hamilton Nisbets to the Ogilvys of
  Inverquharity in 1992.

# OLIPHANT

**Chief of the Name and Arms:**
Richard Eric Laurence Oliphant of that Ilk
**Motto:** 'Provide for all' ('*Tout pourvoir*')
www.clanoliphant.org

The Oliphant family are of Norman origin. Having taken part in William the Conqueror's invasion of England in 1066, they held lands in Northamptonshire where they were associated with David I and rescued him from capture at the Rout of Winchester in 1141.

David, godson of David I, received the lands of Crailing and Smailholm in Roxburghshire. In 1296, Sir William Oliphant of Aberdalgie, having fought at the Battle of Dunbar, held Stirling Castle during the siege of Edward I of England. Robert the Bruce rewarded the Oliphants with the land of Gask and Aberdalgie. Sir William's son, Sir Walter, married Princess Elizabeth, youngest daughter of King Robert I. The title of Lord Oliphant appears to have been granted several times, but in 1751 the peerage became extinct after the death of Lord Oliphant of the de facto third creation.

The 4th Lord Oliphant fought for Mary, Queen of Scots at the Battle of Langside in 1568 and several branches of the clan supported the Jacobite Risings of 1689, 1715 and 1745. The Chiefship having become dormant, in 2003, Richard Eric Laurence Oliphant of that Ilk was recognised by the Lord Lyon King of Arms as Chief of the Name and Arms of Oliphant.

## ANCESTRAL INTEREST

Ardblair Castle, Blairgowrie, PH10 6SA. Tower house dating from 16th century. Passed from Blairs to Oliphants of Gask in 1792 and remains the family home of the Blair Oliphants.

OLIPHANT MODERN

Hatton Castle, Newtyle, Angus, PH12 8UN. Lands given to Sir
    William Olifard by Robert the Bruce in 1317. Castle built in
    1575. Restored and now a private home.
Kellie Castle, Pittenweem, Anstruther, KY10 2RE. Assigned to
    Walter Olifard of Abergeldie c.1360 and occupied by the
    Oliphant family for 250 years. Now in the portfolio of
    National Trust for Scotland.
Old House of Gask, Auchterarder, PH3 1HP. Home of the
    Oliphants of Newton. It was plundered by the English after
    the Battle of Culloden in 1746. Later became the childhood
    home of 19th-century poet Carolina Oliphant, Lady Nairn.

# PRINGLE

**Chief of the Name and Arms:** Sir Norman Murray MacGregor Pringle of that Ilk and Stichill, 10th Baronet
**Motto:** 'Friendship gives honour' (*Amicitia reddit honores*)
www.jamespringle.co.uk

This family dates from the reign of Alexander III, taking its surname from Hoppringle on the Gala Water. In the 14th century the Pringles held lands around Galashiels and were squires to the earls of Douglas. Having fought at the Battle of Otterburn in 1388, Robert Pringle was granted a charter for the lands of Smailholm in Roxburghshire. David Pringle, son of the Laird of Smailholm, was killed with his four sons at the Battle of Flodden in 1513.

Sir James Pringle of Smailholm is said to have been obliged to sell off land to pay off the debts he incurred at the court of James VI. The Pringles of Torwoodlee were Covenanters and offered shelter to those being persecuted for their faith. Thomas Pringle, the poet and writer, was born in Teviotdale and in 1827 was appointed Secretary to the Anti-Slavery Society.

The last Hoppringle of that Ilk, Pringle of Torsonce on the Gala Water, died in 1737 and his only daughter, Margaret, married Gilbert Pringle, son of the Nova Scotia Baronet of Stichill, thus carrying the Pringle estates and arms into that branch of the family. In 2020, Sir Norman Murray Pringle of Stichill was recognised by the Lord Lyon King of Arms as Chief of the Name and Arms of Pringle.

## ANCESTRAL INTEREST

The Haining, Selkirk, TD7 5LR. Country house and estate that belonged to the Pringle family from c.1790. Bequeathed to the people of Selkirk and run by the Haining Charitable

Trust. Outhouses have been converted into studios. Birthplace of Old Ginger, ancestor of the popular Dandie Dinmont breed of terrier.

Old Gala House, Galashiels, TD1 3JS. An impressive mansion dating from 1583 and held by the Pringle Lairds of Galashiels. It is now a museum and art gallery

Smailholm Tower, Kelso, TD5 7PG. Built in the 15th century for the Pringle family and designed to protect against sporadic English raids. Historic Environment Scotland.

Torwoodlee Tower, Galashiels, TD1 1UB. Built in 1601 to replace a tower that had been destroyed by Clan Elliot and Clan Armstrong in 1568.

# RAMSAY

**Chief of the Name and Arms:**
The Rt Hon. James Ramsay, 17th Earl of Dalhousie
**Motto:** 'Pray and work' ('*Ora et labora*')
**Plant Badge:** Blue harebell
www.clanramsay.org

This Anglo Norman family was first recorded in
Scotland when granted lands in Lothian by David
I. By the 13th century there were five major
branches of Ramsay: Dalhousie, Auchterhouse,
Banff, Forfar and Clatto. In 1400, Dalhousie
Castle was attacked by the English but so well
defended that the English were obliged to
withdraw. In 1513, Sir Alexander Ramsay was killed at the Battle
of Flodden.

Sir John Ramsay of Dalhousie and Melrose was created Lord
Ramsay of Melrose in 1618, and William, 2nd Baron of Melrose,
was created Earl of Dalhousie in 1633 in acknowledgement of his
involvement in the battles of Marston Moor and Philiphaugh.

The 9th Earl of Dalhousie served as Governor General of
British North America from 1819 to 1828, and the 10th Earl of
Dalhousie was Governor-General of India from 1847 to 1856. In
1919, Queen Victoria's granddaughter, Princess Patricia of
Connaught and Strathearn, married Alexander Ramsay, son of
the 14th Earl of Dalhousie. The 16th Earl was Governor General
of Rhodesia and Nyasaland from 1957 to 1963 and Lord
Chamberlain to Queen Elizabeth The Queen Mother.

The Ramsays of Bamff, who acquired a Nova Scotia
baronetcy in 1666, are descended in the male line from Neis de
Ramsay, physician to Alexander II.

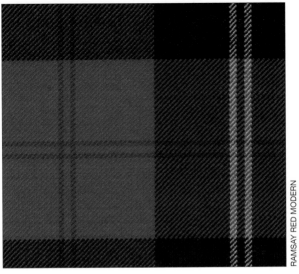

RAMSAY RED MODERN

## ANCESTRAL INTEREST

Brechin Castle, Angus, DD9 6SG. Acquired through marriage
into the powerful de Maule family. Bamff House, Alyth,
PH11 8LF. Built as a fortified tower in the 16th century.
Family home of Ramsays of Bamff and now run as an eco
estate.

Dalhousie Castle, Midlothian, EH19 3JB. This was the Ramsay
stronghold in the 13th century and is now a hotel.

# RATTRAY

**Chief of the Name and Arms:** Lachlan Rattray of Rattray
**Motto:** 'My wishes are above the stars' (*Super sidera votum*)
www.clanrattray.com

The Rattrays were followers but not a sept of the Murrays of Atholl. The surname is taken from the Barony of Rattray in Perthshire and the family descends from Adam de Rattrief who lived in the 13th century.

During the Wars of Scottish Independence, Eustace Rattray was captured at the Battle of Dunbar in 1296 and taken to England. His grandson Alexander sat in the Ayr Parliament which determined the succession to the Scottish throne in 1315. Silvester Rattray of Rattray was Ambassador to England in 1463 and inherited the Fortingal estates from his mother, thus causing a rift with the Stewart earls of Atholl, and in 1533, Patrick Rattray was murdered by one of their followers. David Rattray was a staunch Royalist who fought for Charles II at Worcester in 1651 and was held prisoner in the Tower of London.

A charter of novodamus for the Rattray lands was granted under the Great Seal in 1648, uniting the baronies of Kinballoch and Rattray into one free barony of Craighall.

RATTRAY ANCIENT

**ANCESTRAL INTEREST**

Craighall Castle, Rattray, Blairgowrie, PH10 7JB. Sixteenth-
century stronghold of Clan Rattray perched high above the
River Ericht. Sold in 2010 and privately owned.

# ROBERTSON (DONNACHAIDH)

**Chief of the Name and Arms:**
Gilbert Robertson of Struan, 24th Chief of Clan Donnachaidh
**Motto:** 'Glory is the reward of valour' (*'Virtutis gloria merces'*)
**Plant Badge:** Bracken
www.donnachaidh.com

Duncan or Donnachaidh Reamhair ('Stout Duncan'), who led the clan for Robert the Bruce at the Battle of Bannockburn in 1314, claimed descent from the Celtic Mormaers of Atholl. From a later chief in the reign of James I comes the surname Robertson.

The Barony of Struan was granted to Robert Duncanson by James II for capturing Sir Robert Graham who had assassinated his father. Thereafter the Robertsons feuded with their neighbours, the Stewarts of Atholl. A substantial amount of Robertson lands were sold off but later recovered by John Robertson, a wealthy Edinburgh merchant who conveyed them to the Robertsons of Struan.

As staunch Royalists, the Robertsons rallied to the banner of the Marquis of Montrose and took part in all of the Jacobite Risings. As a result their estates were forfeited. The Barony of Struan was returned by the Crown in 1784 but was sold by George, 18th Chief, in 1854.

ROBERTSON RED MODERN

## ANCESTRAL INTEREST

Auchinleeks House, Pitlochry, PH18 5UF. Built in the early 19th
    century for Robert Robertson. Privately owned.

Clan Donnachaidh Museum, House of Bruar, Pitlochry,
    PH18 5TW. Opened in 1969.

Dunalastair Castle, Pitlochry, PH16 5PB. Ruined original seat of
    Clan Robertson overlooking eastern end of Loch Rannoch.
    Although privately owned, the estate incorporates the
    ancestral Robertson burial ground.

Eilean nam Faoileag, Loch Rannoch. Site of island castle of the
    Robertsons of Struan.

# ROSE

**Chief of the Name and Arms:** David Rose, 26th of Kilravock
**Motto:** 'Constant and true'
**Plant Badge:** Wild rosemary
www.rosefamilyassociation.com

The Norman family of Rose of Kilravock settled in the Moray Firth area in the reign of David I. In 1290, Marie de Bosco, heiress to Kilravock, married Hugh de Ros. The Roses of Kilravock supported Robert the Bruce in the Wars of Scottish Independence, taking part in the capture of Invernairn Castle in 1306.

In the 14th century, Hugh Rose married the daughter of the constable of Urquhart Castle on Loch Ness. The Rose family supported the Reformation and led the clan against the Marquis of Montrose at the Battle of Auldearn in 1645. However, when Charles I was handed over to the English Parliament, Rose of Kilravock raised a regiment of dragoons to rescue him.

In 1715, the Roses supported the British Government against the Jacobites and Arthur Rose was killed leading the clan to seize Inverness. However, on the eve of the Battle of Culloden in 1746, Prince Charles Edward Stuart was entertained at Kilravock while the Duke of Cumberland occupied the Rose town house at nearby Nairn. In 2013, David Rose was acknowledged by the Lord Lyon King of Arms as Chief of Clan Rose.

ROSE HUNTING ANCIENT

## ANCESTRAL INTEREST

Kilravock Castle, Nairn, IV2 7PJ. Ancestral largely 17th-century
mansion house of the Rose family. Both Mary, Queen of
Scots and her son James VI stayed here. Run by Kilravock
Christian Trust.

# ROSS

David Campbell Ross of Ross and Balnagown
**Motto:** 'Success nourishes hope' (*Spem Successus Alit*)
**Plant Badge:** Juniper
www.clanross.org

This clan is descended from Fearchar Macin Taggart, son of the priest of the Monastery of Applecross, who helped Alexander II to crush a rebellion by the son of Donald Bain, his rival to the Scottish throne. In 1215, for his services, he was knighted and recognised as Earl of Ross. In the next generation, his son William received grants of lands on Skye and Lewis.

During the Wars of Scottish Independence, Clan Ross fought against the English at the Battle of Dunbar in 1296 and Battle of Bannockburn in 1314. The 5th Earl was killed at the Battle of Halidon Hill in 1333. In the 15th century, both the Ross chief and Mackay chief were killed in a feud and their successors were summoned before the Earl of Argyll to make peace.

John, 2nd Lord Ross, died at the Battle of Flodden in 1513, and Clan Ross fought side by side with Clan Munro to defeat the Royalist army of the Marquis of Montrose. The two clans similarly fought together during Jacobite Risings although Malcolm Ross of Pitcalnie supported the Old Pretender in the 1715 Rising. In 1968, the chiefship passed to David Ross of Ross and Shandwick, a descendant in the male line of Fearchar Macin Taggart.

**ANCESTRAL INTEREST**

Balnagown, Invergordon, IV18 0NU. Castle built by the Rosses
in 1375 but lost in the 18th century until bought back by the
Rosses of Hawkhead, a southern branch of the clan. The
property remained with the family until 1978 when it was
purchased by Mohamed Al-Fayed. A selection of luxury
lodges, cottages and houses can be leased.

# SCOTT

**Chief of the Name and Arms:** His Grace Richard Scott,
10th Duke of Buccleuch and 12th Duke of Queensberry
**Motto:** 'I love' ('*Amo*')
**Plant Badge:** Blaeberry
www.clanscottscotland.com

The Latin word *Scotti* was used to describe the
ancient Celts of Ireland. However, the earliest
surviving record of the surname was that of
Uchtred 'Filius Scott' in a charter of c.1120. His
two sons are claimed as the ancestors of the Scotts
of Buccleuch, and Sir Michael Scott, the famous
wizard of the Scotts of Balweary.

The Scotts were supporters of Robert the Bruce during the
Scottish Wars of Independence. From Sir Michael Scott descend
the Lords Polwarth. With their stronghold at Branxholme Castle,
the Scotts were at their most influential as a Border clan in the
16th century.

The Lordship of Scott of Buccleuch was created in 1606 and
the earldom in 1619. In 1633, the daughter of Francis, 2nd Earl of
Buccleuch, Countess of Buccleuch in her own right, married
James, Duke of Monmouth, natural son of Charles II. On their
marriage they were created Duke and Duchess of Buccleuch,
each in their own right. Although Monmouth was subsequently
beheaded for treason against his uncle James VII and II, the
Buccleuch title passed to their eldest son. A later marriage linked
the Buccleuch family with the wealthy Douglas dukes of
Queensberry.

Several Scott clansmen fought for the British Government
during the Jacobite Rising of 1745. The great Scottish novelist Sir
Walter Scott, author of *Ivanhoe* and *The Lay of the Last Minstrel*,
was descended from the Scotts of Harden.

### ANCESTRAL INTEREST

Abbotsford House, Melrose, TD6 9BQ. Residence of Sir Walter Scott between 1817 and 1825. Open to public.

Aikwood Tower, Selkirk, TD7 5HJ. Border peel tower built in 1535. Purchased and restored by Lord Steel in early 1990s.

Bowhill House and Country Estate, Selkirk, TD7 5ET. Purchased by 2nd Duke of Buccleuch in 1747. Remains the Borders residence of current Duke.

Branxholme Castle, Hawick, TD9 0JT. Owned by Clan Scott since 1420.

Kirkhope Tower, Selkirk, TD7 5JW. Sixteenth-century residence of the Scotts of Harden. Privately owned.

# SCRYMGEOUR

**Chief of the Name and Arms**
The Rt Hon. Alexander Scrymgeour, the 12th Earl of Dundee
**Motto:** 'Dissipate'
**Plant Badge:** Rowan
www.scrimgeourclan.org.uk

Two documents issued in 1296 by William Wallace and Robert the Bruce confirm the clan lands in Fife on behalf of the Crown and Realm of Scotland. These bestowed upon Alexander Schrymeschur, son of Colin, son of Carun, the perilous but honourable privilege of carrying the King's banner in war, the office of constable of the Castle of Dundee, and certain lands in the Dundee neighbourhood. Later grants were made of lands near Inverkeithing and further lands were acquired through marriage to the heiress of Glassary in Argyll.

John Scrymgeour of Glassary carried the Royal banner at the Battle of Flodden in 1513. He was fatally wounded. In 1641, another John Scrymgeour was created Viscount Dudhope and Baron Scrymgeour of Inverkeithing. The 3rd Viscount Dudhope, a Royalist, was created Earl of Dundee in 1660. On his death without heir, his estates were seized for the Crown. However, in 1686, these estates passed to John Graham of Claverhouse who two years later was created Viscount Dundee. Claverhouse died at the Battle of Killiecrankie in 1689 whereupon his estates passed to Clan Graham.

David Scrymgeour of Kirkton, sheriff of Inverness, married Catherine Wedderburn of Wedderburn and their son assumed the additional surname. At the coronation of Edward VII, Henry Scrymgeour-Wedderburn carried the standard of Scotland. In 1953, his grandson was recognised as 11th Earl of Dundee by the House of Lords.

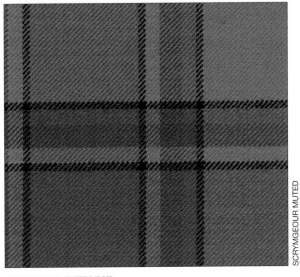

**ANCESTRAL INTEREST**

Birkhill Castle, Cupar, KY15 4QP. Seat of the earls of Dundee.
   Private home.
Dudhope Castle, Dundee, DD3 6TU. Built after the Battle of
   Bannockburn to replace Dundee Castle. Seat of Scrymgeours
   but acquired by Grahams of Claverhouse in 1683.

# SEMPILL

**Chief of the Name and Arms:** The 21st Lord Sempill
**Motto:** 'Keep tryst'

 A Renfrewshire family since the 13th century when Robert de Sempill witnessed a charter to Paisley Abbey. They supported Robert the Bruce during the Wars of Scottish Independence and received lands in Renfrewshire and Ayrshire, where they became hereditary sheriffs. John Sempill was created Lord Sempill by James IV and in 1505 founded the Collegiate Church of Lochwinnoch, building Castle Semple at the far end of the loch. He was killed at the Battle of Flodden in 1513.

John's grandson Robert was a faithful supporter of Mary, Queen of Scots until the death of Lord Darnley, whereupon he transferred his allegiance to her son James. His son John Sempill of Beltrees was married to Mary Livingston, one of Queen Mary's maids of honour. He remained a Catholic and was castigated by the Reformer John Knox as 'Sempill the dancer'.

Lord Sempill supported the Regent Moray at the Battle of Langside in 1568 and was rewarded with a charter for the abbey lands of Paisley. The Sempills supported the Royalist cause during the Civil War and as a result they were fined by the Commonwealth. The 10th Lord Sempill fiercely opposed the Act of Union in 1707. Ironically, his younger brother, 12th Lord Sempill, commanded the left wing of the Hanoverian Army at the Battle of Culloden.

SEMPILL

## ANCESTRAL INTEREST

Castle Semple, Lochwinnoch, Renfrewshire, PA12 4HJ. Ruined
Sempill Castle peel tower in Clyde Muirshiel Regional Park.

Craigievar Castle, Alford, AB33 8JF. Completed by Aberdonian
merchant William Forbes in 1626, the castle passed into the
Forbes-Sempill family through marriage. Gifted to the
National Trust for Scotland in 1963.

# SHAW

**Chief of the Name and Arms:** Ian Shaw of Tordarroch
**Motto:** 'By fidelity and fortitude' ('*Fide et fortitudine*')
**Plant Badge:** Red whortleberry
www.theclanshaw.org

Shaw MacDuff, a younger son of the Thane of Fife and descendant of King Kenneth MacAlpine, was made keeper of Inverness Castle by Malcolm IV of Scotland. His sons became known as the 'sons of the Thane'. His grandson was granted lands at Rothiemurchus in the 13th century and his son Farquhar allied himself through marriage with Clan Donald.

Farquhar's son was Angus Mackintosh who married the daughter of the Chief of Clan Chattan, and their younger son was John Angus, 1st Chief of Clan Shaw. In the 14th century, an ongoing feud between Clan Mackintosh and Clan Comyn led the Shaws to support Robert the Bruce in his claim to the Scottish throne and they fought on his behalf at the Battle of Bannockburn in 1314.

The Shaws took part in the Battle of the North Inch in Perth fought between Clan Chattan and Clan Cameron in 1396. Some clansmen, but not all, supported the Jacobite cause in 1715 and 1745. In 1970, Major Ian Shaw of Tordarroch was recognised by the Lord Lyon King of Arms as Chief of Clan Shaw.

SHAW

**ANCESTRAL INTEREST**

Doune of Rothiemurchus, Aviemore, PH22 1QP. Built by Clan
Comyn and passed to Clan Shaw but lost in 1542 to the
Gordons before being acquired by the Grants.

Tordarroch Castle, Inverness, IV2 6XF. Ruined fortification held
by Shaws from 1468 and replaced by Tordarroch House.

# SINCLAIR

**Chief of the Name and Arms:**
The Rt Hon. Malcolm Sinclair, 20th Earl of Caithness
**Motto:** 'Commit thy work to God'
**Plant Badge:** Whin
www.clansinclair.org

The St Clairs from Normandy arrived in Scotland with Princess Margaret Aetheling in 1068. She became the second wife of Malcolm III and after her death was canonised by the Pope. William 'The Seemly' St Clair was rewarded with the baronies of Roslin and Pentland in Midlothian. The St Clairs built Rosslyn Castle and Abbey and, in 1160, a younger son was granted the lands of Herdmanston in Haddingtonshire.

During the Wars of Scottish Independence, the Sinclairs supported Robert the Bruce, and Sir William Sinclair was among the knights who accompanied the heart of King Robert to the Holy Land. In 1379, Sir Henry Sinclair claimed the earldom of Orkney through his mother from Haakon VI of Norway. It was later exchanged with James III for the earldom of Caithness. William Sinclair, 2nd Earl of Caithness, was killed with 300 Sinclairs at the Battle of Flodden in 1513. The Sinclairs subsequently fought at the battles of Summerdale on Orkney and Solway Moss. Henry, 6th Lord Sinclair, assisted Mary, Queen of Scots in her escape from Loch Leven Castle. The clan also assisted the Marquis of Montrose at the Battle of Carbisdale in 1650 and supported the Jacobite cause in the 1715 Rising, but transferred allegiance to the Hanoverian Government in 1745.

SINCLAIR RED MODERN

## ANCESTRAL INTEREST

Castle Sinclair Girnigoe, Wick. Cliff-top Sinclair ruin.

Dunbeath Castle, Caithness, KW6 6EB. Seventeeth-century
Sinclair tower. Privately owned.

Keiss Castle, Caithness, KW1 4XB. Partially ruined 18th-century
Sinclair castle near to ruins of Old Keith Castle
(16th century).

Rosslyn Castle, Roslin, EH25 9PX. Partially ruined 14th-century
castle with accommodation through Landmark Trust.

Rosslyn Chapel, Roslin, EH25 9PU. Founded by Sir William
St Clair in 1446. Restored as a visitor attraction and
interdenominational church.

# STIRLING

**Chief of the Name and Arms:** Francis Stirling of Cadder
**Motto:** 'Gang forward'
www.clanstirling.com

The Stirling surname derives from the town of that name and first appears in the 12th century. Around 1147, the name Thoraldus appears in a charter of David I for the lands of Cadder, and his descendant Sir Alexander de Strivelyn, 5th Laird of Cadder, is on record as having died in 1304. Sir John de Strivelyn died fighting against the English army at the Battle of Halidon Hill in 1333.

James I appointed Sir William Strivelyn Governor of Dumbarton Castle and he became Comptroller of the Royal Household, a post held in turn by his son and grandson. In 1927, Sir George Stirling of Glorat was appointed keeper of Dumbarton Castle.

The Stirlings acquired the lands of Keir in the mid-15th century and supported James IV in his rebellion against his father. His descendent Sir Archibald Stirling of Keir supported Charles I during the Civil War and, upon the Restoration, he was appointed to the Supreme Court with the judicial title of Lord Garden. The Stirlings of Keir fought for the Jacobites in both the 1715 and 1745 Risings.

STIRLING ANCIENT

## ANCESTRAL INTEREST

Dumbarton Castle, Dumbarton, G82 1JJ. The Stirlings were
  appointed keepers of Dumbarton Castle in 1497, 1510, 1534
  and 1927. Historic Environment Scotland.

Glorat House, East Dunbartonshire, G66 8EL. Nineteenth-
  century baronial home of the Stirlings of Glorat.

Keir House, Dunblane, FK15 9NR. Home of the Stirling family
  from 15th to 20th century. Privately owned.

# SUTHERLAND

**Chief of the Name and Arms:**
Alistair Sutherland, 25th Earl of Sutherland
**Motto:** 'Without fear' ('*Sans peur*')
**Plant Badge:** Cotton sedge
www.clansutherland.org.uk

This clan takes its name from the shire of
Sutherland in the north of Scotland, known by
the Norse invaders as the 'land to the south'.
Freskin, a Flemish nobleman, was progenitor of
Clan Murray. However, his youngest son, Hugh
Freskin, was granted the lands of Sutherland by
William the Lion in 1197.

The Sutherlands supported the Royal House of Stuart and
fought for Robert the Bruce at the Battle of Bannockburn in
1314. The clan was frequently at odds with Clan Sinclair and
Clan Mackay. William Sutherland, 4th of Duffus, was killed at
the Battle of Flodden in 1513. In 1517, Elizabeth, 10th Countess of
Sutherland in her own right, married Adam Gordon, and thus
the earldom and chiefship passed through their son Alexander
Gordon, Master of Sutherland. In the 17th century, John
Gordon, 16th Earl of Sutherland, changed his surname to
Sutherland. The male line then continued until 1771 when the
17th Earl's granddaughter Elizabeth married George Leveson-
Gower, 2nd Marquess of Stafford, who was created 1st Duke of
Sutherland shortly before his death in 1833.

When the 5th Duke died, the chiefship and earldom of
Sutherland passed to the daughter of the 2nd son of the 4th
Duke, and the dukedom passed to a grandson of the 2nd Duke.

SUTHERLAND ANCIENT

## ANCESTRAL INTEREST

Dornoch Castle, Sutherland, IV25 3SD. Built around 1500 for the bishops of Caithness. Gifted to Earl of Sutherland in 1557. It is now the Dornoch Castle Hotel.

Duffus Castle, Elgin, IV30 5RH. Site of Freskin's castle and passed to his Sutherland descendants. Historic Environment Scotland.

Dunrobin Castle, Golspie, KW10 6SF. Family seat of the earls of Sutherland and chiefs of Clan Sutherland. Open to the public.

Helmsdale Castle, Helmsdale, KW8 6JA. Sutherland stronghold. Ruined by 1858.

House of Tongue, Lairg, IV27 4XF. Former seat of Clan Mackay but passed to the Sutherlands in 1829.

# URQUHART

**Chief of the Name and Arms:**
Colonel Wilkins Urquhart of Urquhart
**Motto:** 'Mean well, speak well and do well'
**Plant Badge:** Wallflower

The surname is derived from the lands of Urquhart on Loch Ness. William de Urchard is on record as defending the Moote of Cromarty for William Wallace against the English. From the reign of David II, they served as sheriffs of Cromarty. Sir Thomas Urquhart was knighted by James VI, and his son, another Thomas, was knighted by Charles I.

The Urquharts supported the Jacobite cause in the 1715 Rising but avoided taking part in the Battle of Culloden in 1746. However, a cousin, Adam Urquhart, joined Prince Charles Edward Stuart's court in exile in Rome.

The last of the original chiefly line was Major Beauchamp Urquhart who died in Sudan in 1898. In 1959, the Lord Lyon King of Arms confirmed the Chiefship on Wilkins Trist Urquhart, a descendant of the Urquharts of Braelangswell who had emigrated to the USA in the 18th century.

URQUHART MODERN

**ANCESTRAL INTEREST**

Craigston Castle, Turriff, AB53 5PX. Home of Clan Urquhart
since 1604.

Urquhart Castle, Drumnadrochit, IV63 6XJ. Ruined visitor
attractions. The Urquharts served as early constables.
Historic Environment Scotland.

# WALLACE

**Chief of the Name and Arms:** Andrew Robert Wallace
**Motto:** 'For liberty' (*Pro libertate*)
**Plant Badge:** Oak
www.clanwallace.org

The Waleis were originally Britons from Wales, who settled in the ancient kingdom of Strathclyde, and the name is found in 12th-century records in Ayrshire and Renfrewshire. Richard Wallensis was in the service of Walter Fitz Alan, first Steward of Scotland. His grandson Adam had two sons, Adam, 4th Laird of Riccarton in Ayrshire, and Malcolm, who received the lands of Elderslie and Auchinbothie in Renfrewshire.

Malcolm was the father of Scotland's hero Sir William Wallace who led the revolt against English rule and occupation before his capture and grisly demise in London in 1305, eight years before Robert the Bruce's great victory against Edward II of England on the battlefield of Bannockburn.

After several generations in Jamaica, a family of Wallace came forward as the owners of the Busbie and Clancaird estates in Ayrshire and were recognised by the Lord Lyon King of Arms as Chiefs of the Name and Arms of Wallace.

## ANCESTRAL INTEREST

Craigie Castle, Kilmarnock, Ayrshire, KA1 5PG. Acquired by John Wallace of Riccarton through marriage in 1371.
The National Wallace Monument, Abbey Craig, Stirling, FK9 5LF. Erected by public subscription in 1869 to commemorate Sir William Wallace.

WALLACE RED MODERN

Riccarton Castle, Ayrshire, KA3 2RP. The Wallaces held the
   barony of Riccarton and it was the home of William
   Wallace's uncle. Now a ruin.
Wallace Statue, Aberdeen, AB25 1JY. Sculpted by William Grant
   Stevenson (1849–1919).
William Wallace statue, Melrose, TD6 0RQ. Statue of Scotland's
   hero erected in 1814 near to the ruins of Dryburgh Abbey.

# SEPTS

Many of the surnames of Scotland have been altered in the spelling since first written down. There was no standardisation of spelling and countless variations evolved. Members of the same family often took protection from different clans. In some cases brothers of the same family gave allegiance to different clan chiefs. Invariably the surnames they carried were simply territorial.

Below is a simple guide, but it has to be underlined that some surnames are claimed by more than one clan. Obviously there are many names not included in this list, and the total accuracy of the following connections cannot be guaranteed.

ABBOT MacNab
ABBOTSON MacNab
ADAM Gordon
ADAMSON Shaw and
    Mackintosh
ADIE Gordon
AIRLIE Ogilvy
ALAISTER MacDonald
ALCOCK MacDonald
ALEXANDER MacDonald
    and MacArthur

ALISON MacDonald
ALLAN MacDonald and
    MacFarlane
ALLANSON MacDonald and
    MacFarlane
ALLEN MacDonald
ALLISTER MacDonald
ALPIN MacAlpine
ANDERSON MacDonald and
    Ross
ANDREW Ross

ANGUS MacInnes
ARTHUR Campbell and
    MacArthur
AYSON Mackintosh
AYSON (NZ) Mackintosh and
    Shaw

BAIN MacKay and MacBain
BALLACH MacDonald
BALLOCH MacDonald
BANNATYNE Campbell
BANNERMAN Forbes
BARTHOLEMEW Leslie and
    MacFarlane
BAXTER Macmillan
BAYN MacKay
BEAN MacBain
BEATH MacDonald
BEATON MacDonald,
    Macleod and Maclean
BELL Macmillan and Douglas
BETHUNE MacDonald
BLACK Maclean, Lamont and
    Macgregor
BLACKADDER Douglas
BLACKETT Douglas
BLACKSTOCK Douglas
BOWIE MacDonald
BRIEVE Morrison
BRODIE Brodie and
    MacDonald
BROWN Lamont and Douglas
BROWNLEE Douglas
BUCHAN Comyn
BUDGE MacDonald

BUIE MacDonald
BURNS Campbell
BURNESS Campbell
BURNETT Campbell

CADEL Campbell
CADDELL Campbell
CAIRD Sinclair and
    MacGregor
CALDER Campbell
CALLA MacDonald
CAMBRIDGE MacDonald
CARFRAE Sinclair
CARMICHAEL Carmichael,
    Douglas and MacDougall
CARRISTON Skene
CASKIE Macleod
CATHAL MacDonald
CATHIL MacDonald
CATTANACH Macpherson
CATTEL Campbell
CHALMERS Campbell
CHARLSON Mackenzie
CHEYNE Sutherland
CLARK Macpherson and
    Mackintosh
CLARKE Macpheson and
    Mackintosh
CLERK Macpherson and
    Mackintosh
CLERKSON Macpherson and
    Cameron
CLOUSTON Sinclair
COCHRAN MacDonald
COCHRANE MacDonald

213

COLL MacDonald
COLLYEAR Donnachaidh
COLMAN Buchanan
COLSON MacDonald
COMB MacThomas
COMBIE MacThomas
COMMYN Comyn
CONN MacDonald
CONNACHER MacDonald
CONNAL MacDonald
CONNEL MacDonald
CONNOCHIE Campbell
COOKE MacDonald
COUL MacDougall
COULSON MacDonald
COUTTS Farquharson
COWAN MacDonald and
    Colquhoun
CRAWFORD Lindsay
CREAR Mackintosh
CROCKET Douglas
CROMB MacDonald
CROMBIE MacDonald and
    Gordon
CROOM MacDonald
CRUM MacDonald
CURRIE MacDonald and
    MacPherson

DALLAS Mackintosh
DALYELL Douglas
DANIEL MacDonald
DANIELS MacDonald
DARRACH MacDonald
DARROCH MacDonald

DAVIE Davidson and Clan
    Chattan
DAVIS Davidson and Clan
    Chattan
DAWSON Davidson and Clan
    Chattan
DENOON Campbell
DEUCHAR Lindsay
DEWAR MacNab
DICKSON Douglas
DINGWALL Ross and Munro
DIS Skene
DOCHART MacGregor
DONACHIE Donnachaidh
    (Robertson)
DONALD MacDonald
DONALDSON MacDonald
DONLEAVY Buchanan
DONNELL MacDonald
DONNELSON MacDonald
DONNOCHY Donnachaidh
    (Robertson)
DOUGAL MacDougal and
    Douglas
DOW Davidson and Clan
    Chattan
DRAIN MacDonald
DIFFIE MacFie
DUFFY MacFie
DUNCAN Donnachaid
    (Robertson)
DUNNELL MacDonald
DUNNETT Sinclair
DUNSMORE Murray
DUNUE Campbell

DYCE Skene

EANRIG Gunn
EDIE Gordon
ELDER Mackintosh
ENNIS Innes
ENRICH Gunn
ESSON Shaw and Mackintosh
EWAN MacLachlan
EWEN MacLachlan
EWING MacLachlan

FAIL MacPhail
FALL MacPhail
FARQUHAR Farquharson
FEDERETH Sutherland
FERGUS Fergusson
FERRIES Fergusson
FERSON Macpherson
FINDLAY Farquharson
FINDLAYSON Farquharson
FLEMING Murray
FLETCHER MacGregor
FORDYCE Forbes
FORREST MacDonald
FORESTER DouglaS
FOSTER Douglas
FOULIS Munro

GAIRE Gair
GAINSON Gunn and Sinclair
GALLIE Gunn
GALBRAITH MacDonald and
    Douglas
GALL MacDonald

GALT MacDonald
GAUL MacDonald
GAULD MacDonald
GAYER Gair
GAYRE Gair
GEARE Gair
GEERE Gair
GEORGESON Gunn
GIBB Buchanan
GIBBON Campbell
GIBSON Buchanan and
    Campbell
GILBERTSON Buchanan
GILBRIDGE MacDonald
GILCHRIST Ogilvy
GILFILLAN MacNab
GILL MacDonald
GILLANDERS Ross
GILLESPIE Macpherson
GILLON Macpherson
GILMORE Morrison
GILROY Grant
GLEN Mackintosh
GLENDINNING Douglas
GORRIE MacDonald
GORRY MacDonald
GOULD MacDonald
GOW Macpherson
GOWAN MacDonald
GOWANS MacDonald
GRAY Sutherland
GREGOR MacGregor
GREGORSON MacGregor
GREGORY MacGregor
GREYSACK Fergusson

GRIER MacGregor
GRIGOR MacGregor
GRIMMOND MacLeod
GRUER MacGregor

HALLYARD Skene
HAMILTON Douglas
HANNA Hannay
HANNAH Hannay
HARDIE Fergusson and
    Mackintosh
HARDY Fergusson and
    Mackintosh
HARKNESS Douglas
HARPER Buchanan
HARPERSON Buchanan
HARRES Campbell
HARRIS Campbell
HASTINGS Campbell
HAWES Campbell
HAWSON Campbell
HAWTHORN MacDonald
HEGGIE Mackintosh
HENDERSON Gun and
    MacDonald
HENDRIE MacDonald
HENDRY MacNaughton and
    MacDonald
HENRY MacDonald
HERON MacDonald
HEWISON MacDonald
HOUSTON MacDonald
HOWAT MacDonald
HOWE MacDonald
HOWIE MacDonald

HOWISON MacDonald
HUDSON MacDonald
HUGHSON MacDonald
HUNTLY Gordon
HUTCHEON MacDonald
HUTCHESON MacDonald
HUTCHIN MacDonald
HUTCHISON MacDonald
HUTCHON MacDonald
HUTSON MacDonald

INCHES Donnachaidh
    (Robertson)
INNIS Innes
ISAAC MacDonald and
    Campbell
ISAACS MacDonald and
    Campbell
ISLES MacDonald
IVERSON Campbell

JAMIESON Gunn
JEFFREY MacDonald
JOHNSON MacDonald and
    Gunn
JOHNSTONE MacDonald

KAY Davidson and Clan
    Chattan
KEAN MacDonald and Gunn
KEEGAN MacDonald
KEENE MacDonald
KEITH Sutherland
KELLAR Campbell
KELLER Campbell

KELLY MacDonald
KENDRICK MacNaughton
KENNETH Mackay
KENNETHSON Mackay
KETCHEN MacDonald
KILPATRICK Colquhoun and
Douglas
KINNEL MacDonald
KING MacGregor
KIRKPATRICK Colquhoun
and Douglas
KISSACK Campbell
KISSOCK Campbell

LACHLAN MacLachlan
LANG Gair, Leslie and
Donnachaidh (Robertson)
LAING Gair and
Donnachaidh (Robertson)
LAMB Lamont
LAMBIE Lamont
LAMONDSON Lamont
LANDERS Lamont
LEAN Maclean
LECHY MacGregor
LECKIE MacGregor
LECKY MacGregor
LEES Macpherson
LEITCH MacDonald
LENNY Buchanan
LEYS Farquharson
LINKLATER Sinclair
LOBBAN Logan
LORNE Campbell
LOUDON Campbell

LOVE Mackintosh
LOWDON Campbell
LUCAS Lamont
LUKE Lamont
LYON Farquharson

MACACHIN MacDonald
MACADAMS MacGregor
MACADIE Fergusson
MACAICHAN MacDonald
MACALDINE Lamont
MACALDONISH Buchanan
MACALLAN MacDonald
MACANDEOIR MacNab
MACANDREW Mackintosh
or Ross
MACANGUS Innes
MACARA MacGregor and
MacRae
MACARTAIR Campbell and
MacDonald
MACARTER MacArthur
MACARTHUR Campbell and
MacDonald
MACAULAY Macleod
MACAUSELAN Buchanan
MACAY Shaw and Mackintosh
MACBAXTER Macleod
MACBEATH MacBain,
MacDonald and Maclean
MACBETH MacBain and
Maclean
MACBHEATH MacDonald
MACBRAYNE MacDonald
and MacNaughton

MACBRIDE MacDonald
MACBRIEVE Morrison
MACBURIE MacDonald
MACCAA MacDonald
MACCAIG Farquharson and
   Macleod
MACCAINSH Innes
MACCAIRN MacDonald
MACCALMAN Buchanan
MACCALMONT Buchanan
MACCALLUM Macleod
MACCAMBRIDGE
   MacDonald
MACCARDNEY Farquharson
   and Mackintosh
MACCARRON MacDonald
MACCARTER MacDonald
MACCAW MacDonald
MACCAY MacDonald
MACCEOL MacNaughton
MACCHLERIC Cameron and
   Macpherson
MACCHLERY Campbell,
   Mackintosh and
   Macpherson
MACCLUSKIE MacDonald
MACCLYMONT Lamont
MACCOLM MacThomas
MACCOMAS MacThomas
MACCOMBIE MacThomas
MACCOMISH MacThomas
MACCONNACHER
   Macdougall
MACCONNAL MacDonald
MACCONNECHY Campbell

MACCONNEL MacDonald
MACCONNELLY
   Mackintosh
MACCONNOCHIE
   Campbell
MACCORKILL Gunn
MACCORMACK Buchanan
MACCORMICK MacLaine of
   Lochbuie
MACCOSHAM MacDonald
MACCOWAN Colquhoun,
   MacDonald and
   Macdougall
MACKOY Mackay
MACCULLOCH Macdougall,
   Munro and Ross
MACCUNN Macqueen
MACCURIE MacDonald
MACCURRACH MacDonald
MACCURACK MacDonald
MACCUTCHEN MacDonald
MACCUTCHEON
   MacDonald
MACDADE Davidson
MACDAVID Davidson
MACDERMID Campbell
MACDERMOTT Campbell
MACDIARMID Campbell
MACDERMOTT Campbell
MACDIARMID Campbell
MACDONNACHIE
   Donnachaidh (Robertson)
MACDOWALL
   MacNaughton
MACDOWELL MacDougall

MACELLER Campbell
MACELVER Campbell
MACELVIE Campbell
MACERACHER
    Farquharson
MACEVER Campbell
MACEWAN MacLachlan
MACEWEN MacLachlan
MACFADYEN MacLaine of
    Lochbuie
MACFADZEAN MacLaine of
    Lochbuie
MACFAIL MacPhail
MACFARQUHAR
    Farquharson
MACFAUL MacPhail
MACFERGUS Fergusson
MACGERUSICK Buchanan
MACGIBBON Buchanan and
    Campbell
MACGILBERT Buchanan
MACGILCHRIST Ogilvy and
    MacLachlan
MACGILLEDOW Lamont
MACGILLIVOOR
    MacGillivray
MACGILLONE Cameron
MACGILROY Grant and
    MacGillivray
MACGILVRA MacLaine of
    Lochbuie
MACGILIVRAY MacGillivray
MACGLASRICH Campbell
MACGOUGHAN
    MacDougall

MACGOWAN Gow and
    Macpherson
MACGRIUTHER
    MacGregor
MACGROWTHER
    Drummond
MACGRORY Maclaren
MACGRUDER Drummond
    and MacGregor
MACGRUTHER
    MacGregor
MACGRUITTE MacGregor
MACGUBBIN Campbell
MACGUFFIE MacFie
MACGURE Campbell
MACHARDIE Mackintosh
MACHAY Shaw
MACHENDRY
    MacNaughton
MACIAN Gunn
MACIARRAN Grant
MACILDOWIE Campbell
MACILROY Grant
MAILVIAN MacBain
MACILVORA MacLaine of
    Lochbuie
MACINALLY Buchanan
MACINDEOIR Buchanan
MACINDOE Buchanan
MACKINLAY Fergusson
MACINNES Innes
MACINROY Donnachaidh
    (Robertson)
MACISAAC Campbell and
    MacDonald

MACIVER Campbell,
Mackenzie and
Donnachaidh (Robertson)
MACJAMES MacFarlane
MACKAFFIE MacFie
MACKAIMES Gunn
MACKAIL Cameron
MACKEANISH Gunn
MACKEE Mackay
MACKEGGIE Mackintosh
MACKEITH Macpherson
MACKELLAR Campbell
MACKELVIE Campbell
MACKENDRICK
MacNaughton
MACKENDRACH
MacNaughton
MACKERLICKh Mackenzie
MACKERLIE Campbell
MACKERRACHER
Farquharson
MACKERRAN Grant
MACKERRAS Fergusson
MACKERSEY Fergusson
MACKESSACK Campbell
MACKESSOCK Campbell
MACKEY Mackintosh
MACKICHAN MacDougall
MACKIE Mackay
MACKINLAY Macfarlane and
Buchanan
MACKINNEY Mackinnon
MACKINNY Mackinnon
MACKINVEN Mackinnon
MACKISSOCK Campbell

MACKNIGHT MacNaughton
MACLAGGAN Donnachaidh
(Robertson)
MACLAWS Campbell
MACLEHOSE Campbell
MACLEISH Macpherson
MACLEISTER MacGregor
MACLENNY Maclean
MACLERIE Macpherson
MACLISE Macpherson
MACLIVER MacGregor
MACLOOCH MacFarlane
MACLUGASH MacDougall
MACLUKAS MacDougall and
Lamont
MACLULICH MacDougall,
Munro and Ross
MACLURE Macleod
MACMARTIN Cameron
MACMASTER Buchanan
MACMATH Matheson
MACMATHIE Matheson
MACMAURICE Buchanan
MACMORRAN Mackinnon
MACMURCHIE Buchanan
and Mackenzie
MACMURDO Macpherson
MACMURDOCH
Macpherson
MACMURICH Macpherson
MACMURRAY Murray
MACNACHTAN
MacNaughton
MACNAIR Macfarlane and
MacNaughton

MACNAYER MacNaughton
MACNEE MacGregor
MACNEI MacGregor
MACNEALAGE MacNeil
MACNEISH MacGregor
MACNELLY MacNeil
MACNICHOLL Campbell
MACNEMELL MacDougall
MACNIDES MacFarlane
MACNISH MacGregor
MACNITER MacFrlane
MACNIVEN Comyn,
    Mackintosh and
    MacNaughton
MACNOCAIRD Campbell
MACNUYER Buchanan
MACOMISH MacThomas
MACCONACHIE Campbell
MACONIE Campbell
MACORAN Campbell
MACOWEN Campbell
MACPATRICK Lamont and
    MacLaren
MACPAUL MacPhail
MACPETER MacGregor
MACPETRIE MacGregor
MACPHADDEN MacLaine
    of Lochbuie
MACPHAIL Mackay
MACPHAL MacPhail
MACPHAUL MacPhail
MACPHEDRAN Campbell
    and MacAulay
MACPHEDRON MacAulay
MACPHUN Campbell

MACQUATTIE Forbes
MACQUEY Mackay
MACQUOID Mackay
MACQUISTEN MacDonald
MACQUISTON MacDonald
MACRA MacRae
MACRAITH MacRae
MACRANKIN Maclean
MACRATH MacRae
MACRITCHIE Mackintosh
MACROB Gunn and Innes
MACROBBIE Gair,
    Donnachaidh (Robertson)
    and Drummond
MACROBERT Donnachaidh
    (Robertson)
MACROY Maclaren
MACSORLY Cameron and
    Lamont
MACSWAN Macqueen
MACSWEEN Macqueen
MACSWEN Macqueen
MACSWYLE Macqueen
MACTAGGART Ross
MACTARY Innes
MACTAVISH Campbell
MACTEAR Macintyre and
    Ross
MACTHEARLAICH
    Mackenzie
MACUALRIG Cameron
MACURE Campbell
MACVAIL MacKay
MACVANISH Mackenzie
MACVEAG Maclean

221

MACVEAN MacBain
MACVEY Maclean
MACVINISH Mackenzie
MACVICAR MacNaughton
MACWALTER Macfarlane
MACWATT Forbes
MACWATTIE Buchanan
MACWHIRTER Buchanan
MACWILLIAM Gunn and
    Macfarlane
MANSON Gunn
MARIOCH Innes
MARTIN Cameron of
    Erracht
MARWICK Sinclair
MASON Sinclair
MASTERSON Buchanan
MATHIE Matheson
MAUCHLAN MacLachlan
MAVOR Innes
MAXWELL Douglas
MCCOLM MacThomas
MCCUISTON MacDonald
MEADOWS Sinclair
MEIKLEHAM Lamont
MIDDLETON Innes
MILNE Gordon and Ogilvy
MITCHELL Innes
MOORE Campbell
MORAY Murray
MORE Leslie
MORTON Douglas
MOWAY Sutherland
MUIR Campbell
MURCHIE Mackenzie

MURCHISON Mackenzie
MURDOCH Macpherson
MURDOSON Macpherson

NEAL MacNeil
NEIL MacNeil
NEILL MacNeil
NEILSON Mackay
NELSON Gunn
NICOL Macleod
NICOLSON Macleod
NIVEN Comyn,
    MacNaughton and
    Mackintosh
NOBLE Mackintosh
NORMAN Macleod
NORRIE Skene
NORRIS Gair

OCHILTREE Campbell
OLIPHANT Sutherland
ORR Campbell
OYNIE Innes

PARKER Gair
PATRICK Lamont
PATTEN Maclaren
PATTERSON Maclaren
PAUL Cameron, Mackintosh
    and Mackay
PETER MacGregor
PINKERTON Campbell
POLSON Mackay
POTTINGER Sinclair
PRECIOUS Sinclair